Other books by Laura Torbet

Macramé You Can Wear
Clothing Liberation
The Leather Book

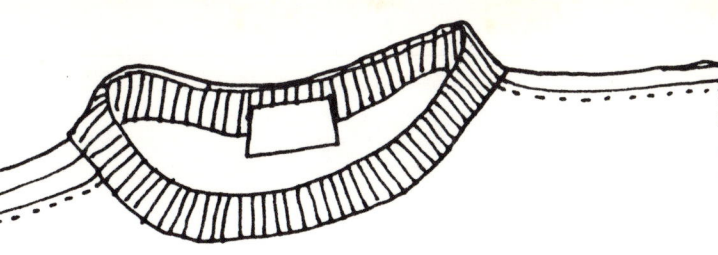

THE
T-SHIRT
BOOK

by Laura Torbet

BOBBS-MERRILL
INDIANAPOLIS / NEW YORK

ISBN 0-672-52228-4
Library of Congress Catalog Card Number: 75-37194
Designed by Helen Barrow
Manufactured in the United States of America

First printing

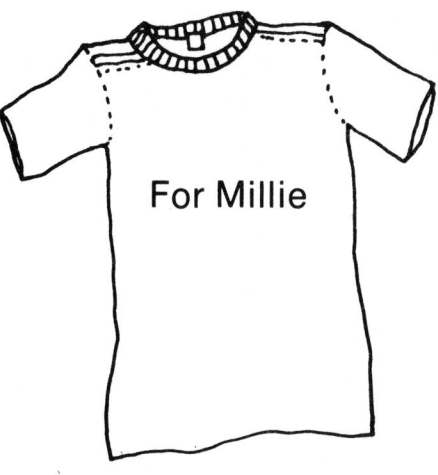

INTRODUCTION

The T-shirt has come into its own. Long a standard, recognized for its comfort and practicality, the T-shirt has now sprung to the height of fashion. This once lowly article of clothing has blossomed into a status item. Yet, of the myriad types available on the market, many are unimaginative, or the ones that everyone is wearing, and those that are unusual tend to be prohibitively expensive. Here is a book full of original designs for you to use to create your own T-shirts, easily and cheaply, and you can adapt and personalize them to create truly unique fashions.

These T-shirts are fun and quick to make. When you read the directions, you'll see how little is involved in the "Torbet T-shirt Technique." Using inexpensive short-sleeved knits sold as men's and boys' undershirts, you can whip up a T-shirt for a friend's birthday, or make something to go with a particular skirt or pair of pants.

Take a T-shirt to lunch today (some designs are especially good for getting into restaurants where a tie is required). And never let on when they ask you who's your tailor.

With thanks to: Keith Buckler
                 Mary Lu Guerra
                 Leonore Fleischer
                 Synnovë Granholm
                 . . . and all the "models."

Laura Torbet

CONTENTS

1.

THE TORBET

T-SHIRT

TECHNIQUE

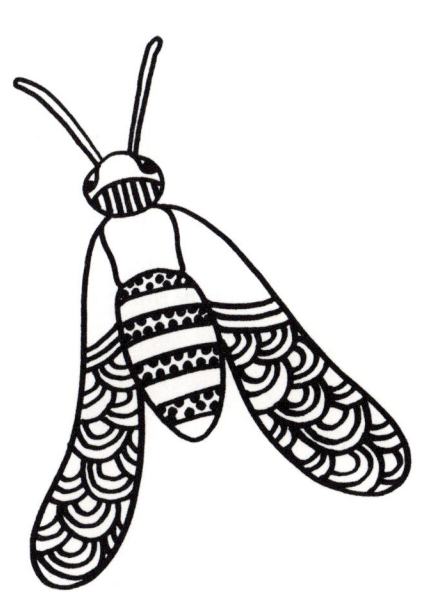

THE TORBET T-SHIRT TECHNIQUE

When it comes to making T-shirts, ''good enough'' is my motto—by which I mean that I like things done well, but done easily, quickly and without too much fuss.

All the T-shirts in this book are done in my favorite medium—permanent felt markers. Markers come in many, many shades, they're easy to work with, produce even color, and can achieve fine lines. And although their color won't last absolutely forever, a markered shirt that's properly cared for will last through many washings before the color fades appreciably.

THE T-SHIRTS

I almost always use plain, common, short-sleeved men's and boys' knit undershirts. Don't worry about sizes—these designs will work for all sizes (as you'll see in the directions that follow). You'll find that a boys' Large or a men's Small size will fit most women. You can also do children's sizes, with slight adjustment, as you'll see.

THE MARKERS

The important thing is to make sure to buy permanent markers. For outlining the design, I use black pointed-tip markers. I prefer a style of marker with a large barrel, yet a fine point—it dispenses more pigment than an ordinary fine line marker and makes an even, strong, easy-to-see line (see ill. 1). Broad-tip permanent markers are best for ''coloring in.'' The best place to buy permanent markers in a wide variety of colors and styles is an art supply store.

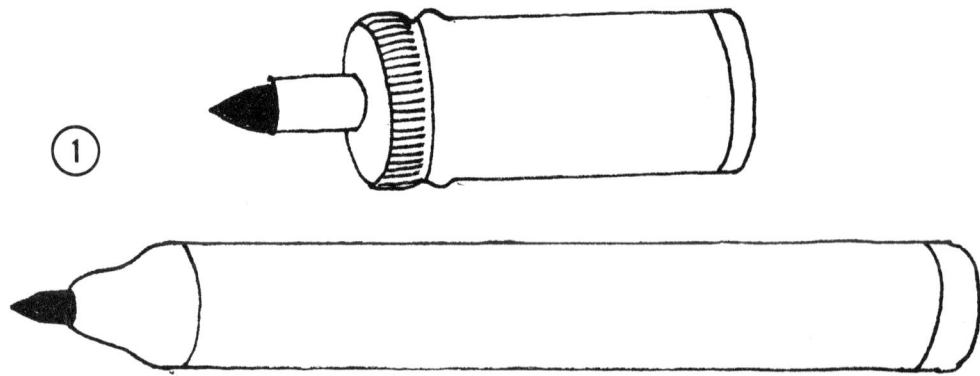

Testing Your Markers

I suggest you test all your markers on a sample piece of cloth and wash it, just to make sure you don't have a "bleeder" in the batch. Especially if you happen to be working with something more precious than a plain undershirt, it's important to anticipate possible disaster with this step.

Using some old piece of white cotton or canvas as your test surface, draw

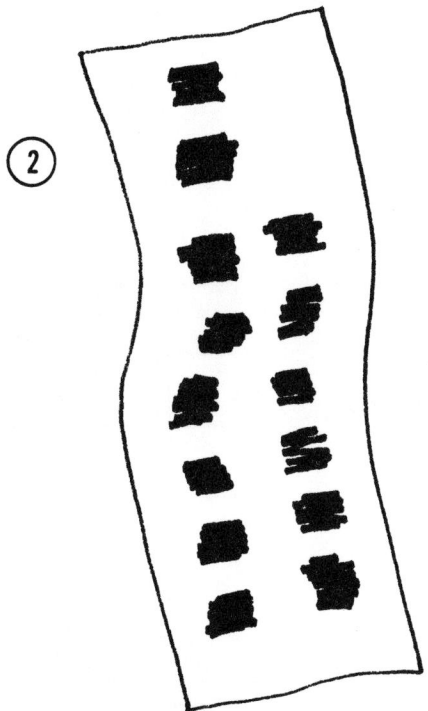

in a strong half-inch square of each color. Press the sample with a hot iron. Soak it for an hour or two in a strong solution of vinegar and cold water, then wash it in cold water with a mild soap. If any color streaks and runs, discard it and try again with another brand. (Even though most will be okay, every brand has some colors that just don't hold as they should. You can't predict beforehand, so this is the only way to make sure.)

When you know your colors are okay, go on and enlarge your design so you can draw it on.

HOW TO ENLARGE THE DESIGN

Your basic tool is a thick cardboard (or any stiff board you have), 18 × 24″, which you use over and over, for all the shirts you marker. This size will work for any T-shirt from a boy's Large to a man's Medium. Men's Large and X-Large sizes can be adjusted to work on this board, as I'll explain. Aside from that you need a sheet of tracing tissue paper big enough to cover the board.

First thing is to draw a 1″ grid on your cardboard—that is, draw horizontal lines 1″ apart, and then vertical lines 1″ apart. Now your grid matches the enlarged size called for in the book, and you'll use it to enlarge all the designs in this book to proper size.

Place your tracing tissue paper over the grid and tape it to the cardboard. You'll see the grid lines clearly through the tracing paper.

Now copy your design onto the tissue, square by square (as in ill. 3), and you're in business. (For children's sizes, see page 16.)

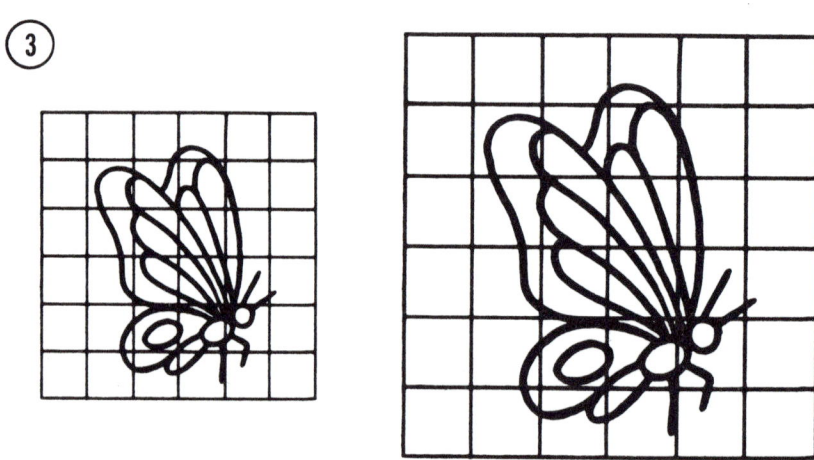

HOW TO TRANSFER THE DESIGN ONTO THE T-SHIRT

The first thing to do is to stretch the T-shirt front over the design board, centering the front over the design you've just enlarged. You'll be able to see the design clearly through the shirt. Center the front of the shirt on the board, lining up the neckline with the dotted line in the design. Check to see that the side seams of the shirt run evenly down the sides of the board. Stretch and tape the sleeves to the back (see ill. 4). Masking tape works best; bulldog clips will also do the job.

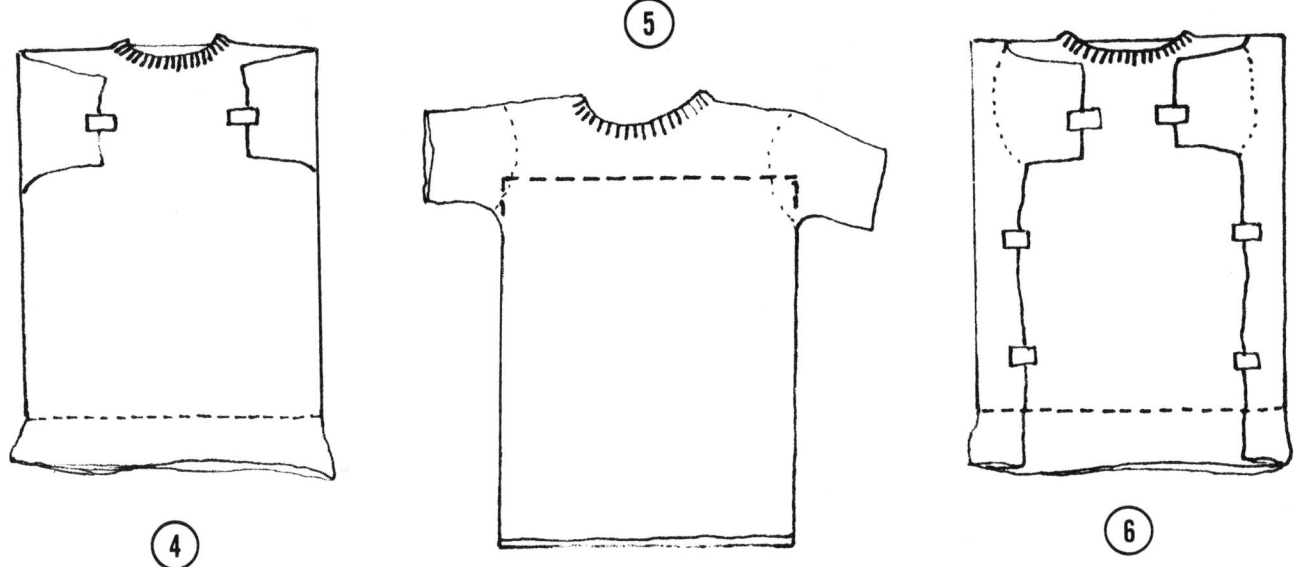

If you are working on a shirt where the motif goes around the bottom, line up the bottom of the shirt with the bottom of the board, and tape in position (see ill. 5). Any design which doesn't have a dotted neckline is meant to be lined up with the bottom of your T-shirt.

As I said earlier, the 18 × 24″ design board will work equally well on boys' Medium and Large and men's Small and Medium sizes: just stretch the smaller sizes to fit over the design board (they'll spring back to shape again afterwards). If you are working on a Large or X-Large men's size, pull the excess material at the sides to the back and tape it so that the material is sufficiently taut to draw on (see ill. 6). When you've traced the basic motif, shuffle the shirt around on your board to continue any lines going out to the sides or down to the bottom of the shirt.

When you're all done, untape the design tracing paper from the cardboard grid and put it away to use another time.

For the back of the shirt, start with another piece of tracing paper, tape it over the cardboard grid and copy the design square by square, just as you did before.

Then stretch the shirt over it again, centering the *back* of the shirt on the board, tape where necessary, and trace as before. Be sure to match up any lines that should connect from the front to the back (collars, waistbands, etcetera).

CHILDREN'S SIZES

For children's sizes, make a smaller design board that their smaller T-shirts will fit over—a 9 × 12″ cardboard for very small sizes, or 12 × 18″ for medium sizes. (For the 9 × 12″ board, a stiff-cover school notebook works well—and you can draw your grid on the back cover.)

Draw your grid lines on the board closer together—make ½″ squares for the 9 × 12″ board, or ¾″ squares for the 12 × 18″ board. Enlarge your design square by square to this smaller size. Then stretch the small T-shirt over its design board and trace exactly as for the larger sizes.

SMALL MOTIFS AND ALPHABETS

You'll also find lots of small motifs and designs—like those on pages 89 and 109—that don't have to be enlarged: just trace and use them same size. And all the alphabets (pages 113 to 123) are drawn to a nice size for T-shirt lettering, so you can trace them as they are to form your words or people's names.

HOW TO DO THE COLORING

Now you are ready to color. If you color with the shirt still on the design board, some of the marker pigment will seep through, so I suggest that you slip the shirt over the reverse of the board for coloring. Don't be concerned about that schooldays' admonition not to go "outside the lines"—the markers tend to spread a little on the fabric as you work. You will quickly learn to control this, but a certain amount of spreading is unavoidable. To control the amount of spread when coloring small sections or near outlines: Use a light touch, and draw close to, but not up to, the outline. The black outline will "catch" the spread. Sometimes a half-dried-up marker comes in handy for coloring small areas.

One caution: do not color in areas around the armpits, as perspiration can cause marker colors to run.

WORKING TIPS AND SUGGESTIONS

For coloring large areas, use a light touch and even strokes, and be sure you're using a marker with lots of color that won't run out on you.

Keep your markers *capped* when not in use.

You can rule or draw lines or circles in pencil as a guide before going over them with the marker. The pencil lines will be covered or will wash out. Don't be afraid to try drawing some of the simpler patterns freehand.

If you are using a knit shirt heavier than a cotton undershirt, or a colored shirt, you probably won't be able to see the lines on the design board clearly enough to trace them. Should you not feel confident enough to copy the design freehand, here are some alternate methods:

Enlarge the design on tracing paper, insert it inside the T-shirt and position it properly. Stretch and tape the T-shirt, with the design inside, to a sunny window, or to a glass tabletop with a lamp positioned underneath, and trace. To color, stretch the shirt over the cardboard (use the reverse for coloring) to hold it taut.

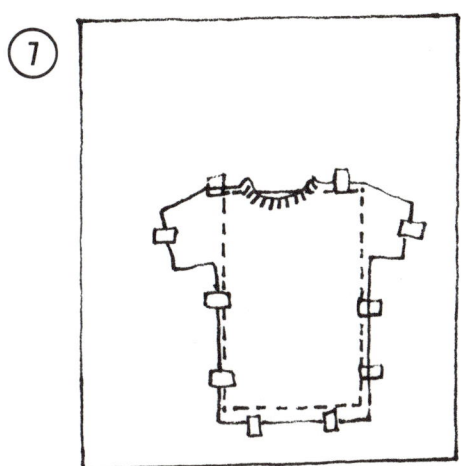

Another technique is to lay the T-shirt over a flat surface and lay dressmaker's carbon (wax side down) over the T-shirt. Lay the enlarged design over the T-shirt and carbon, positioning it carefully, and go over the lines of the design with a stylus, tracing wheel or ball-point pen to transfer the image to the T-shirt.

When working on sleeves or cuffs, you will have to copy the motifs freehand or use one of the methods described above, because the sleeves can't be positioned around the design board. To hold the sleeves taut for drawing and coloring, insert a rolled-up section of newspaper (or folded if it works better), adjusting it until it holds the fabric at the proper tension.

Don't be afraid to improvise. Change and adapt the designs, make use of the individual motifs, switch the fronts and backs of various shirts, add messages and monograms, add your own ideas, be imaginative with color, use different motifs (dots, dashes, squiggles, circles) to fill in large areas.

You can get completely different effects with different color schemes, or by eliminating the outline and just filling in with color. You can simplify some designs by leaving out details, or you can add more elaborate motifs. It's easy to draw freehand on T-shirts, because the fabric gives you a "grain" to follow for straight lines and offers some resistance to the marker, which means you can control the lines easily.

HOW TO PROLONG THE LIFE OF YOUR FINISHED T-SHIRT

This is important, so it's a good idea to follow these suggestions: Before wearing it for the first time, soak it in a strong vinegar and cold water solution. Then wash it in cold water with a mild soap. After this initial treatment, you can throw it in the machine for subsequent washings.

So be bold. Make overall T-shirts for the whole family. Send a bikini to Granny. Send a message to Mary. And have fun.

2.

THE

T-SHIRT

DESIGNS

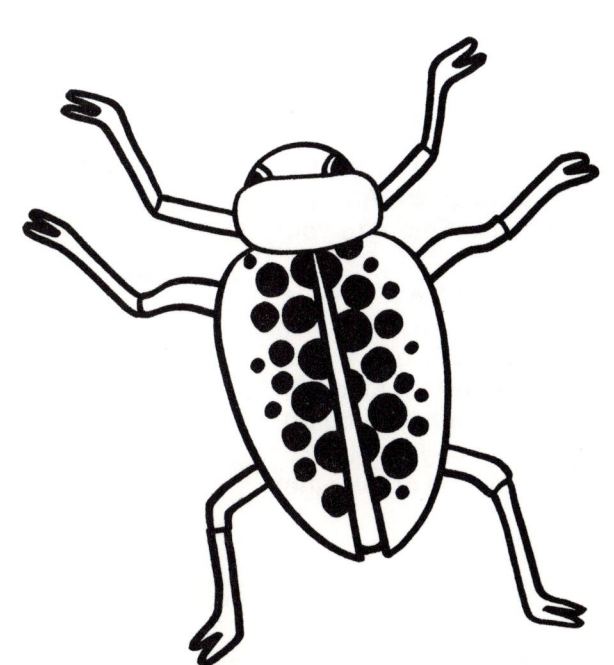

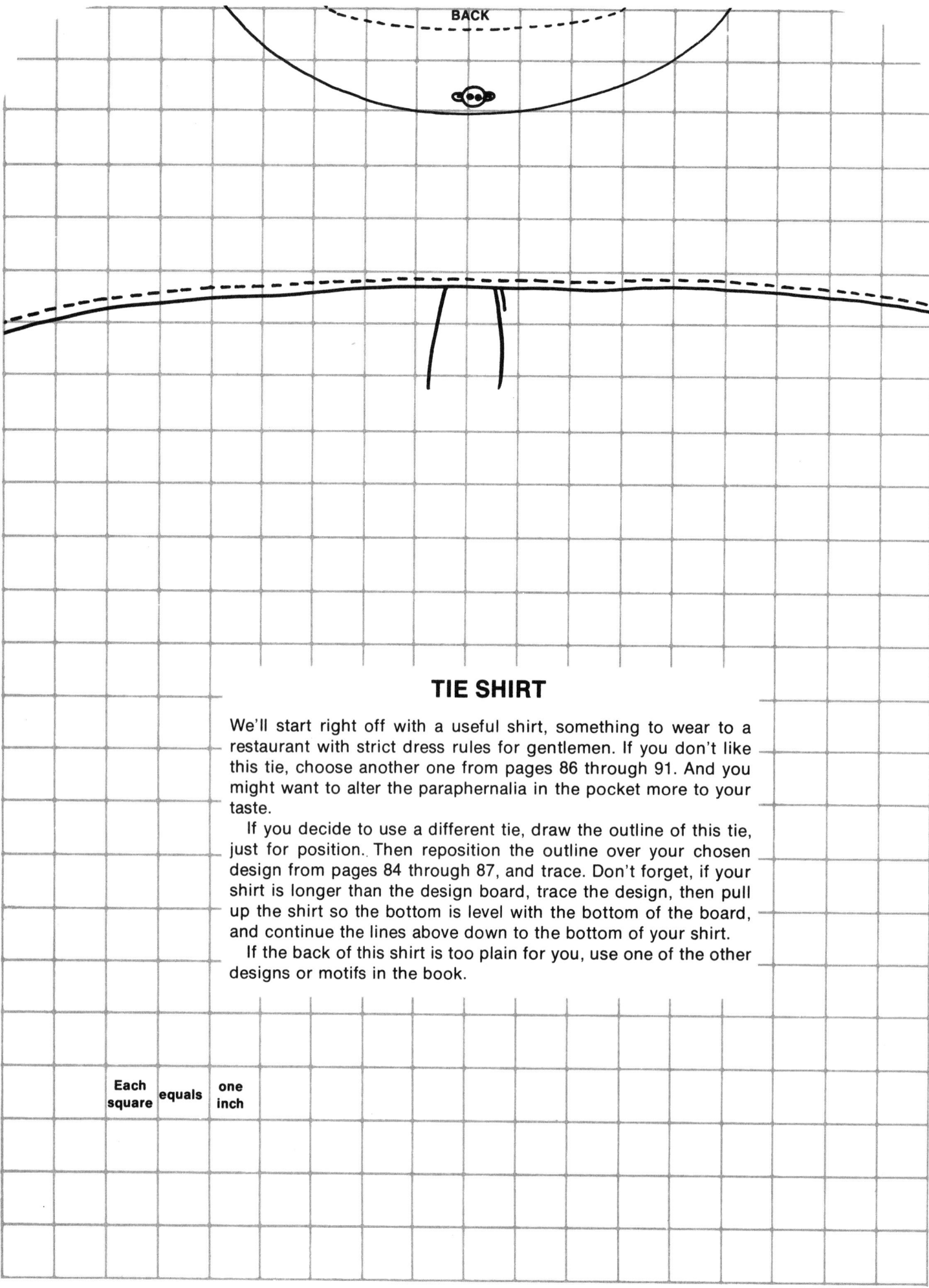

BACK

TIE SHIRT

We'll start right off with a useful shirt, something to wear to a restaurant with strict dress rules for gentlemen. If you don't like this tie, choose another one from pages 86 through 91. And you might want to alter the paraphernalia in the pocket more to your taste.

If you decide to use a different tie, draw the outline of this tie, just for position. Then reposition the outline over your chosen design from pages 84 through 87, and trace. Don't forget, if your shirt is longer than the design board, trace the design, then pull up the shirt so the bottom is level with the bottom of the board, and continue the lines above down to the bottom of your shirt.

If the back of this shirt is too plain for you, use one of the other designs or motifs in the book.

Each square equals one inch

SUN-MOON SHIRT

I drew the outlining circles of this sun-and-moon shirt by using a compass, but it would look just as good done freehand. There are many possible color combinations for this shirt, of course. One suggestion is to color the sun in very bright colors and the moon in more somber night tones.

The moon might be fun with the stripes on its face colored in a rainbow pattern.

FRONT

Each square equals one inch

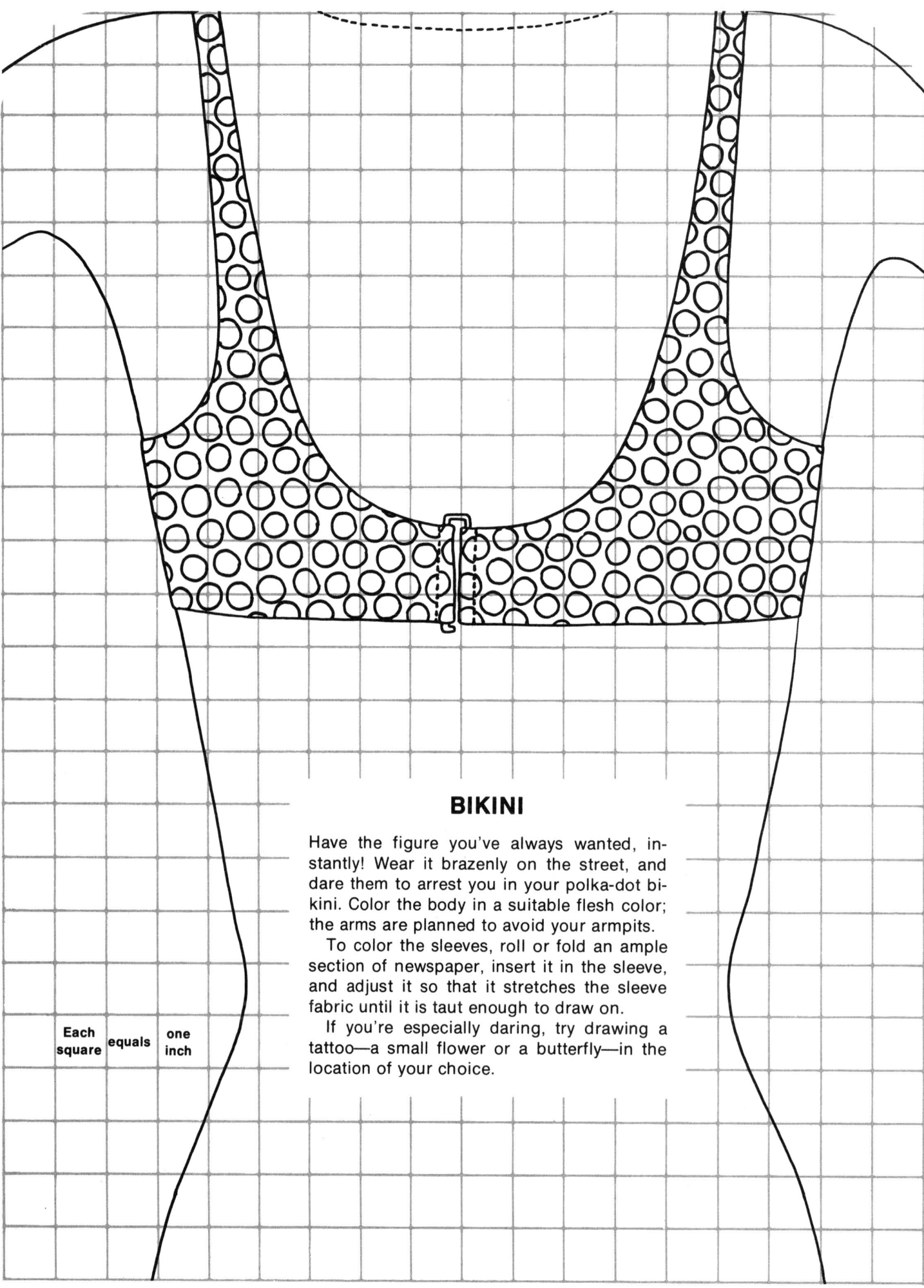

BIKINI

Have the figure you've always wanted, instantly! Wear it brazenly on the street, and dare them to arrest you in your polka-dot bikini. Color the body in a suitable flesh color; the arms are planned to avoid your armpits.

To color the sleeves, roll or fold an ample section of newspaper, insert it in the sleeve, and adjust it so that it stretches the sleeve fabric until it is taut enough to draw on.

If you're especially daring, try drawing a tattoo—a small flower or a butterfly—in the location of your choice.

Each square equals one inch

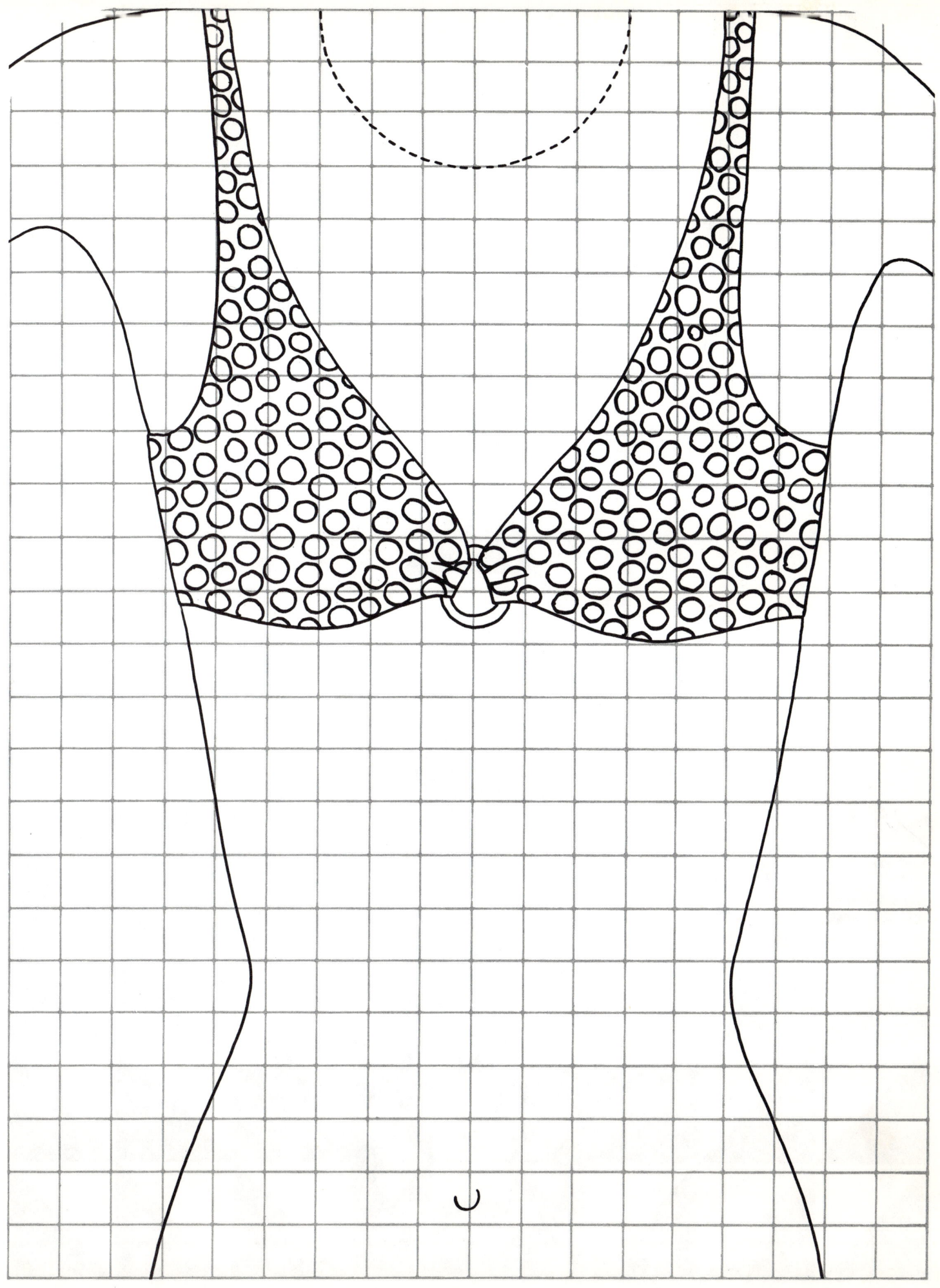

DECO

This Art Deco style design is a fairly elaborate project, but it's quite stunning in living color. Again, you can do this freehand, or use a ruler or compass. You can draw light guide lines with a pencil (the pencil marks will disappear in the wash). For the best effect, have the color follow as definite and symmetrical a pattern as the design.

To position your T-shirt for this design, line up the *bottom* of the shirt with the bottom of the design board, so the design appears as a border at the bottom of the shirt.

You can simplify this pattern in any of a number of easy ways. One way is to do the simple diagonal motif of the larger squares all the way across, eliminating the smaller squares and the triangular top part.

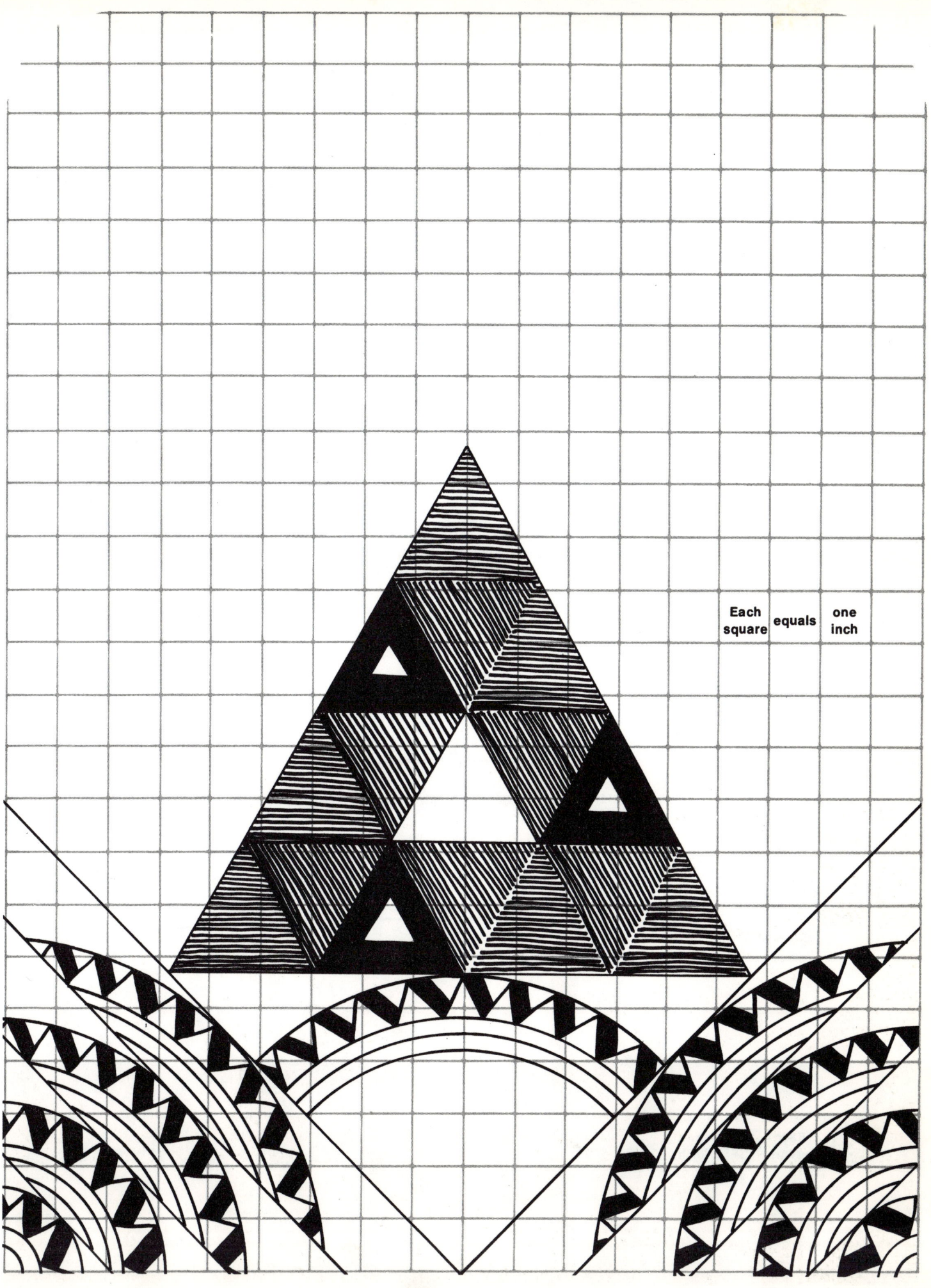

Each square equals one inch

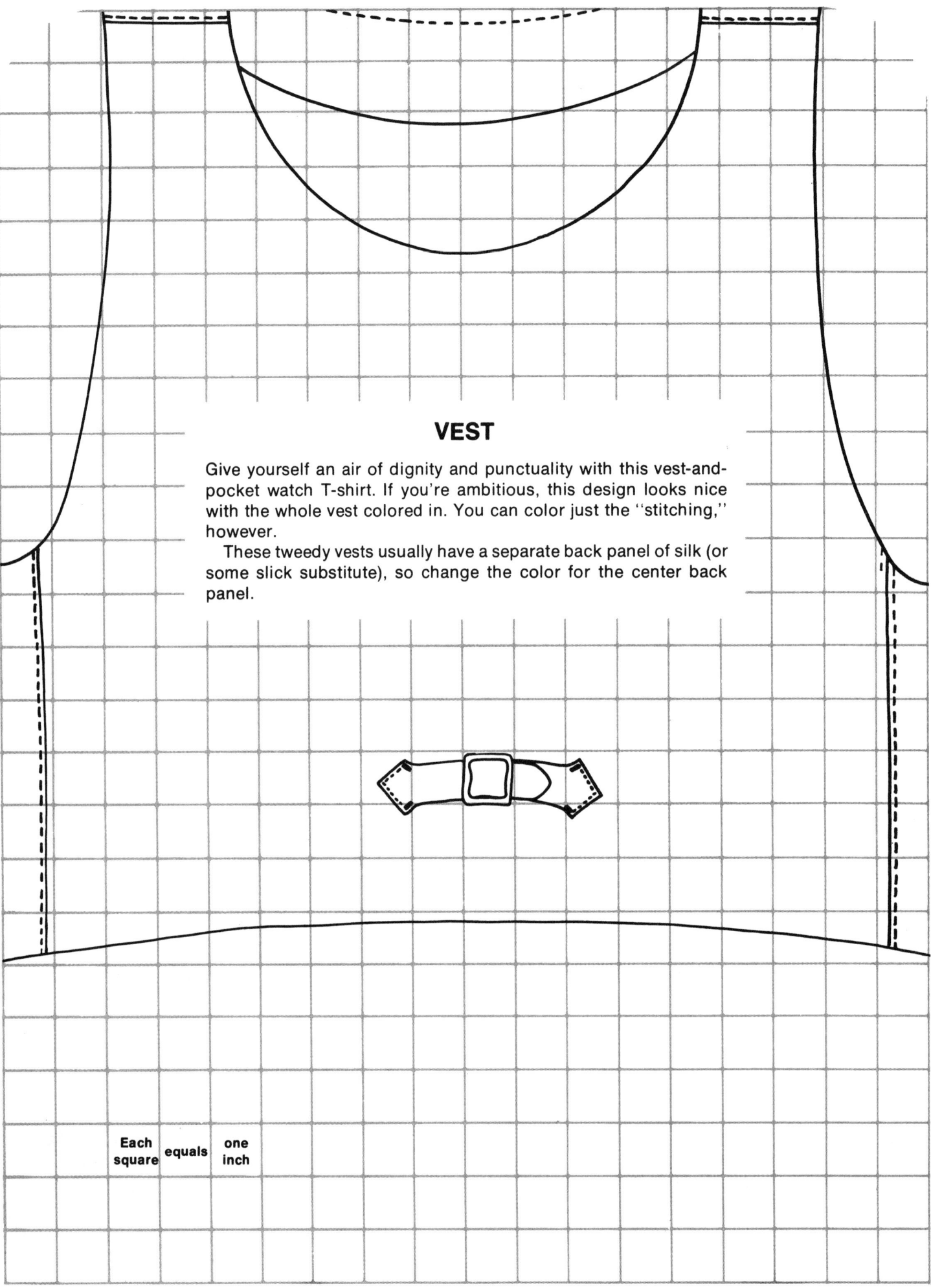

VEST

Give yourself an air of dignity and punctuality with this vest-and-pocket watch T-shirt. If you're ambitious, this design looks nice with the whole vest colored in. You can color just the "stitching," however.

These tweedy vests usually have a separate back panel of silk (or some slick substitute), so change the color for the center back panel.

Each square equals one inch

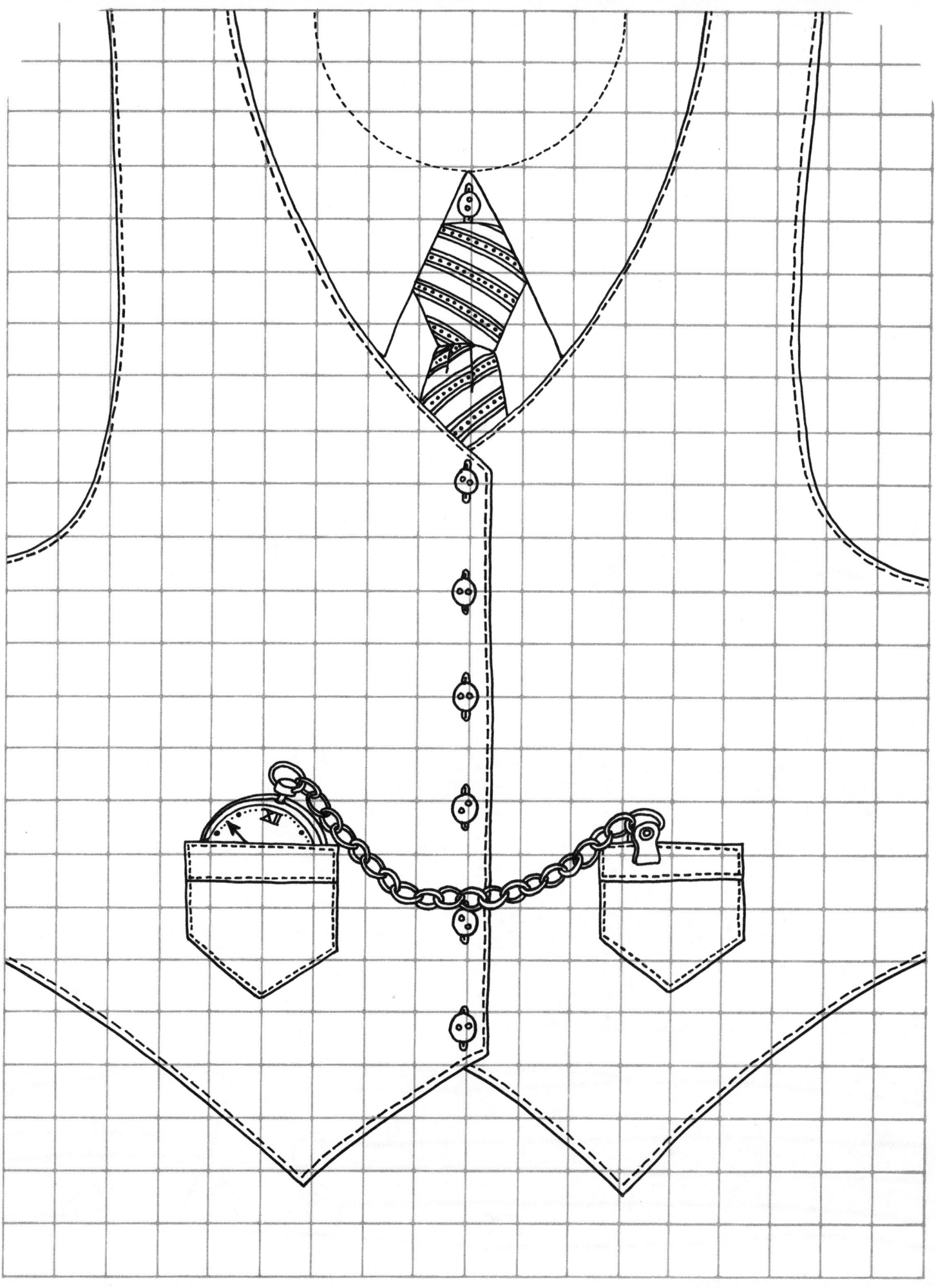

RAIN / SHINE

Here we have the perfect all-weather shirt, "Come Rain or Come Shine." For the correct positioning, line up the bottom of your T-shirt with the bottom of the design board.

To add interest to the design, use several shades of blue and pale green for the water.

For the back, you might color the dots and dashes of rain in two different colors, and do the ground in several tones of green and brown.

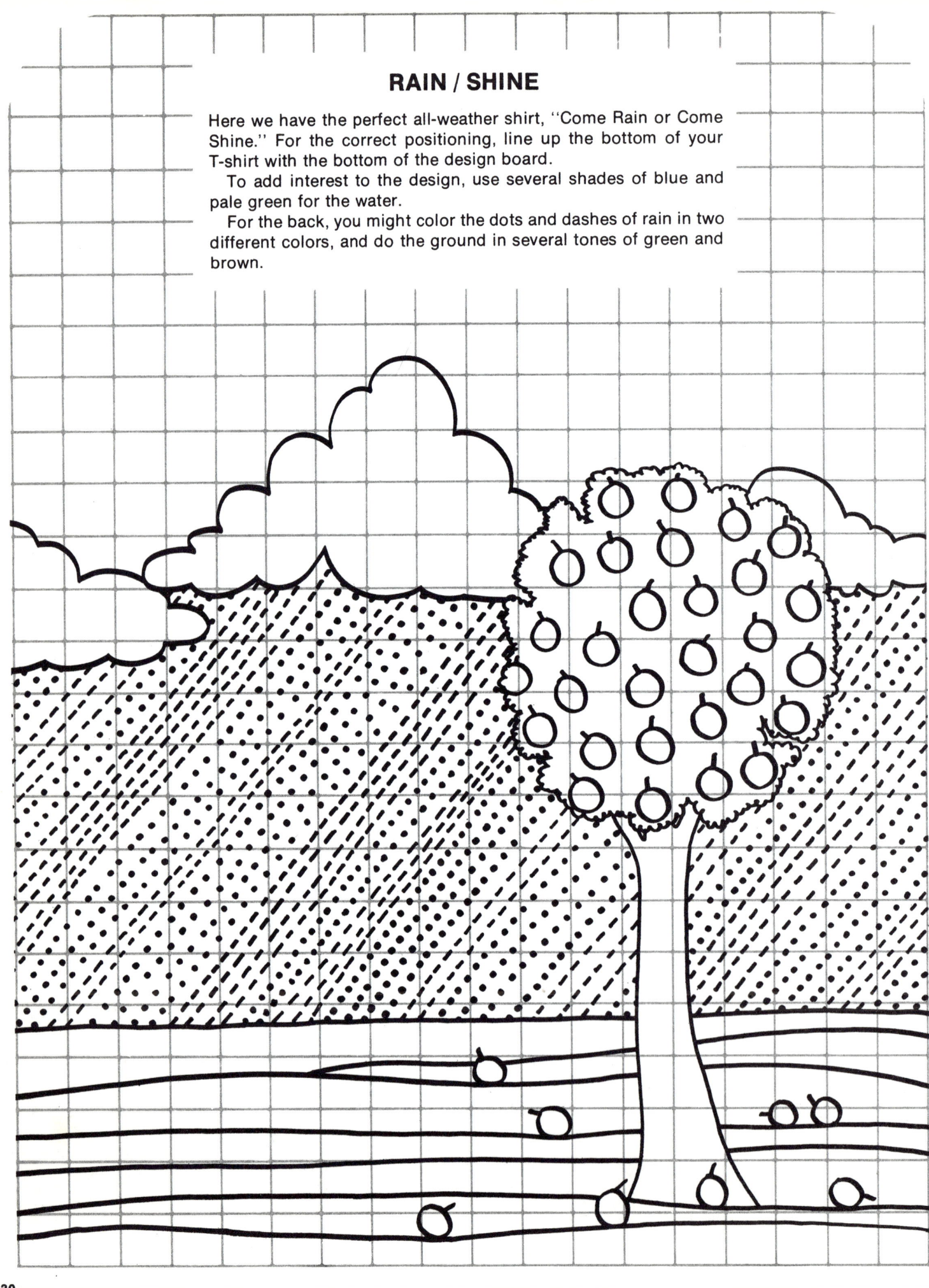

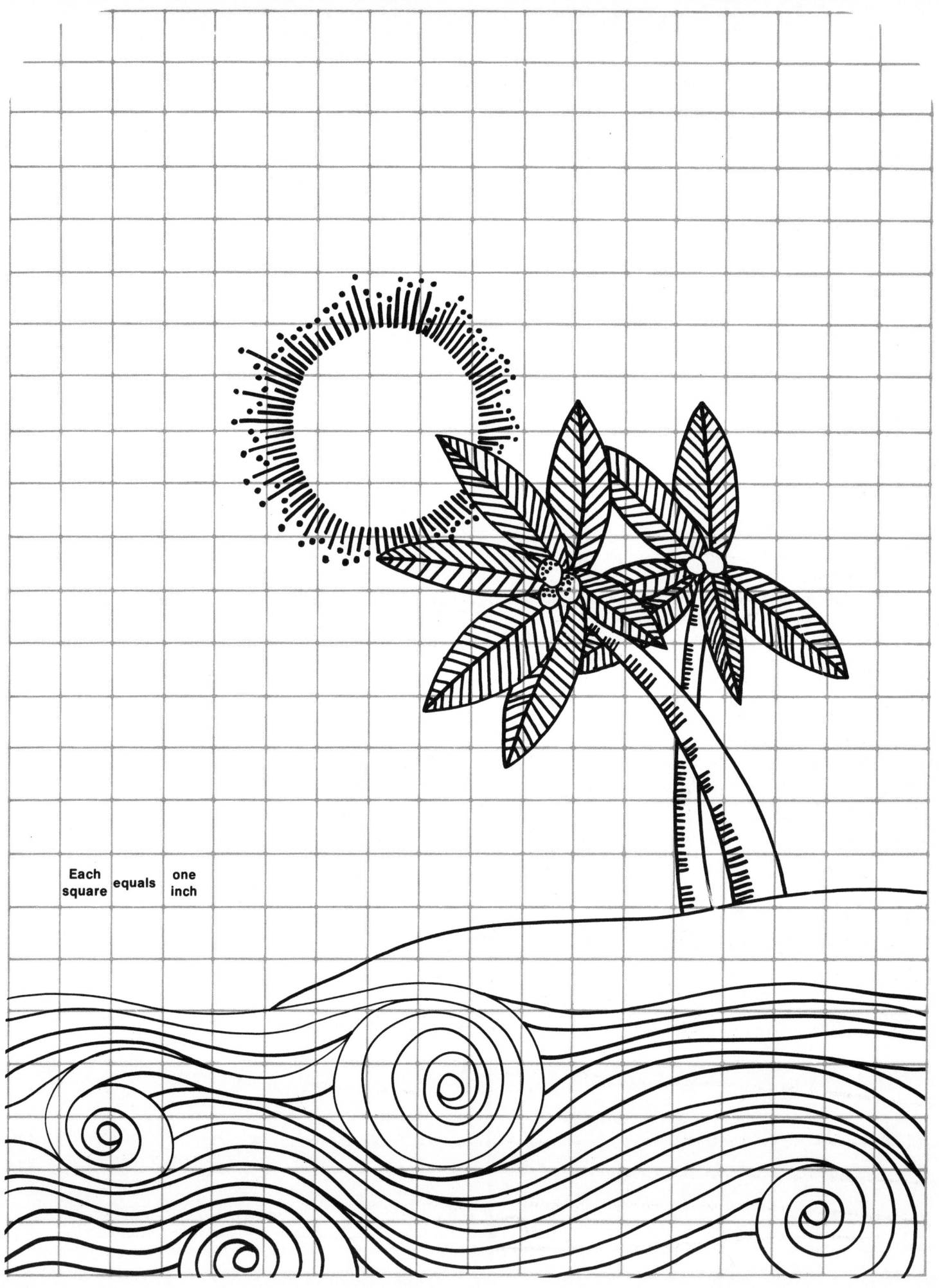

Each square equals one inch

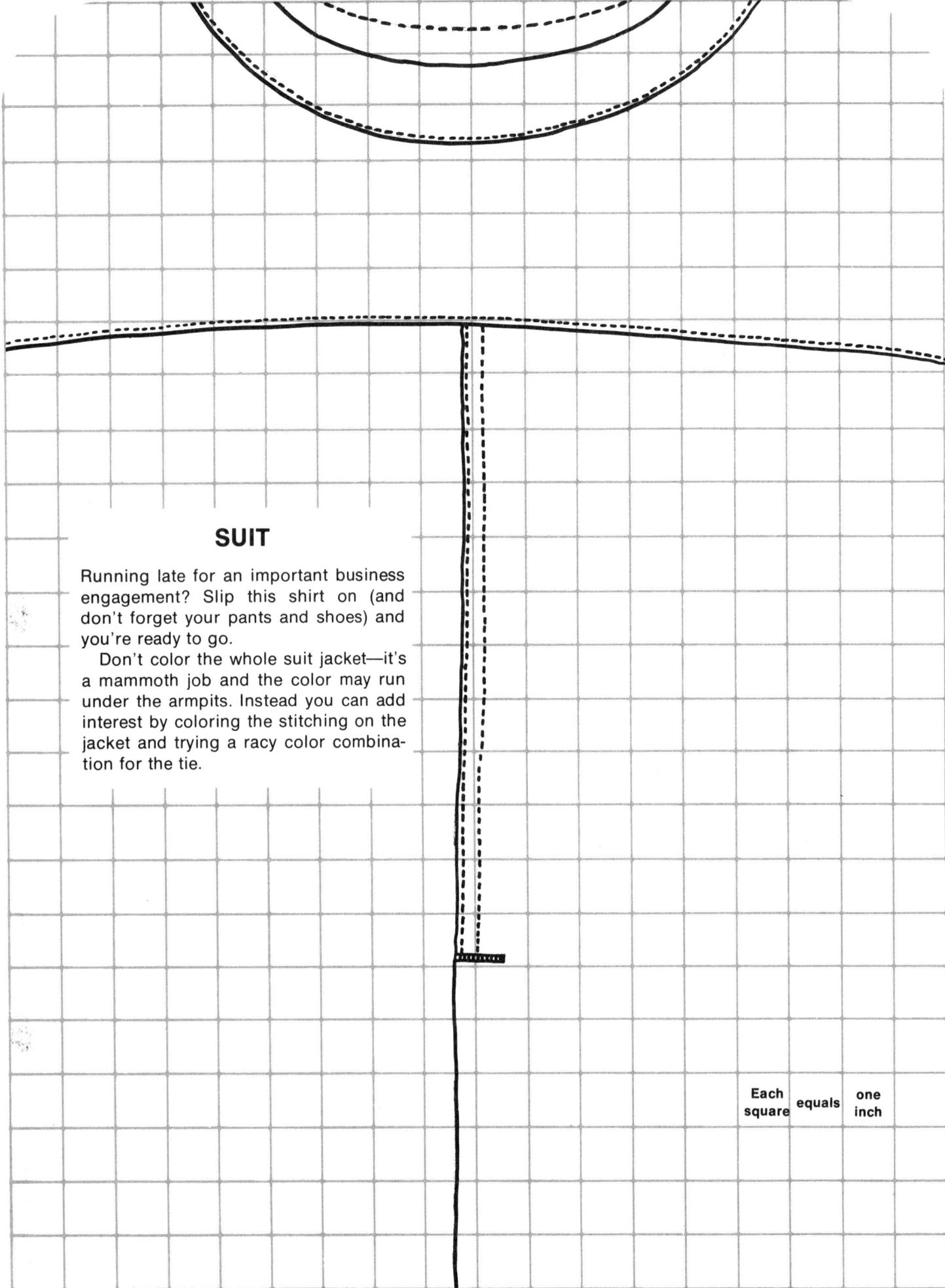

SUIT

Running late for an important business engagement? Slip this shirt on (and don't forget your pants and shoes) and you're ready to go.

Don't color the whole suit jacket—it's a mammoth job and the color may run under the armpits. Instead you can add interest by coloring the stitching on the jacket and trying a racy color combination for the tie.

Each square equals one inch

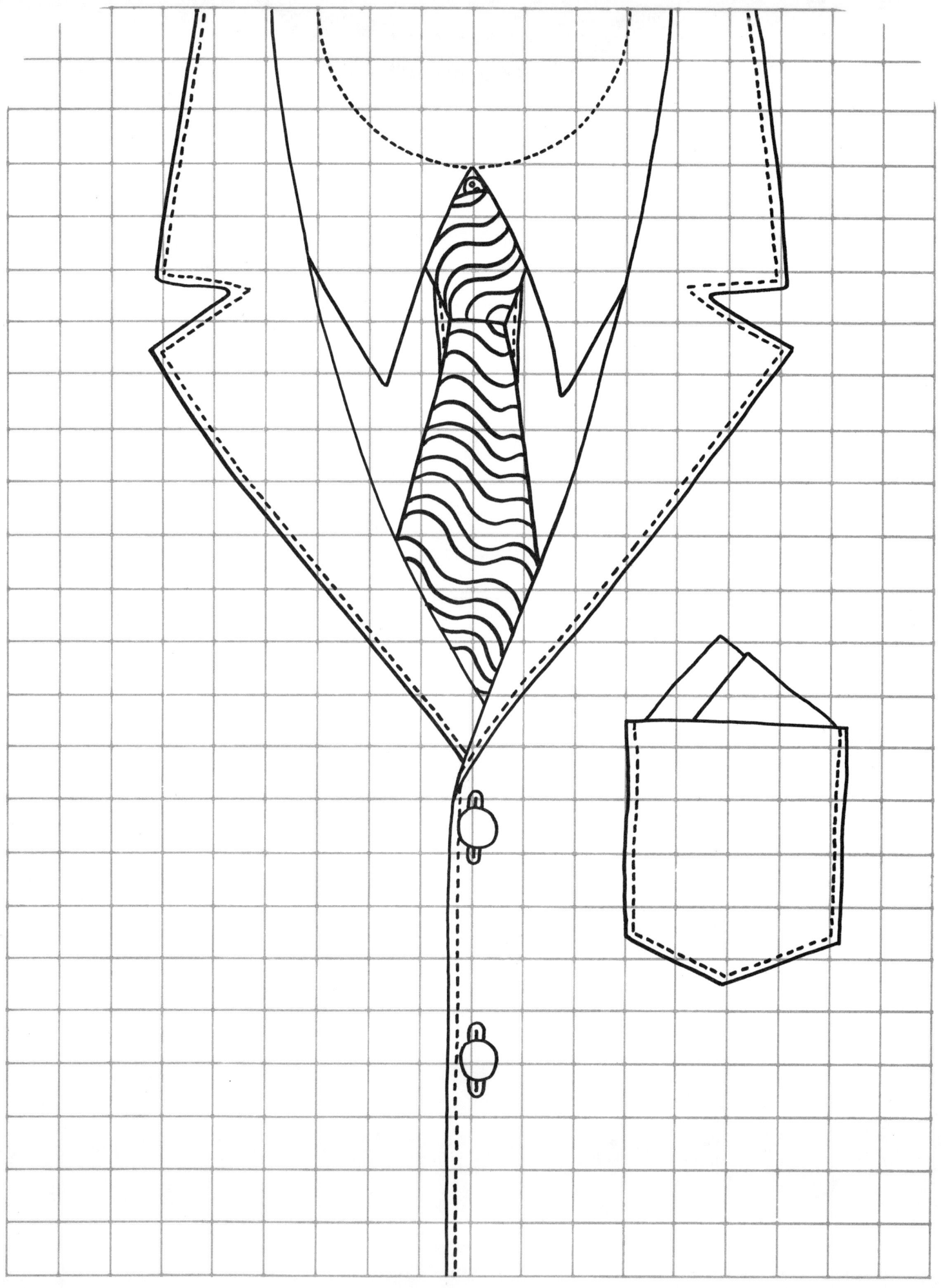

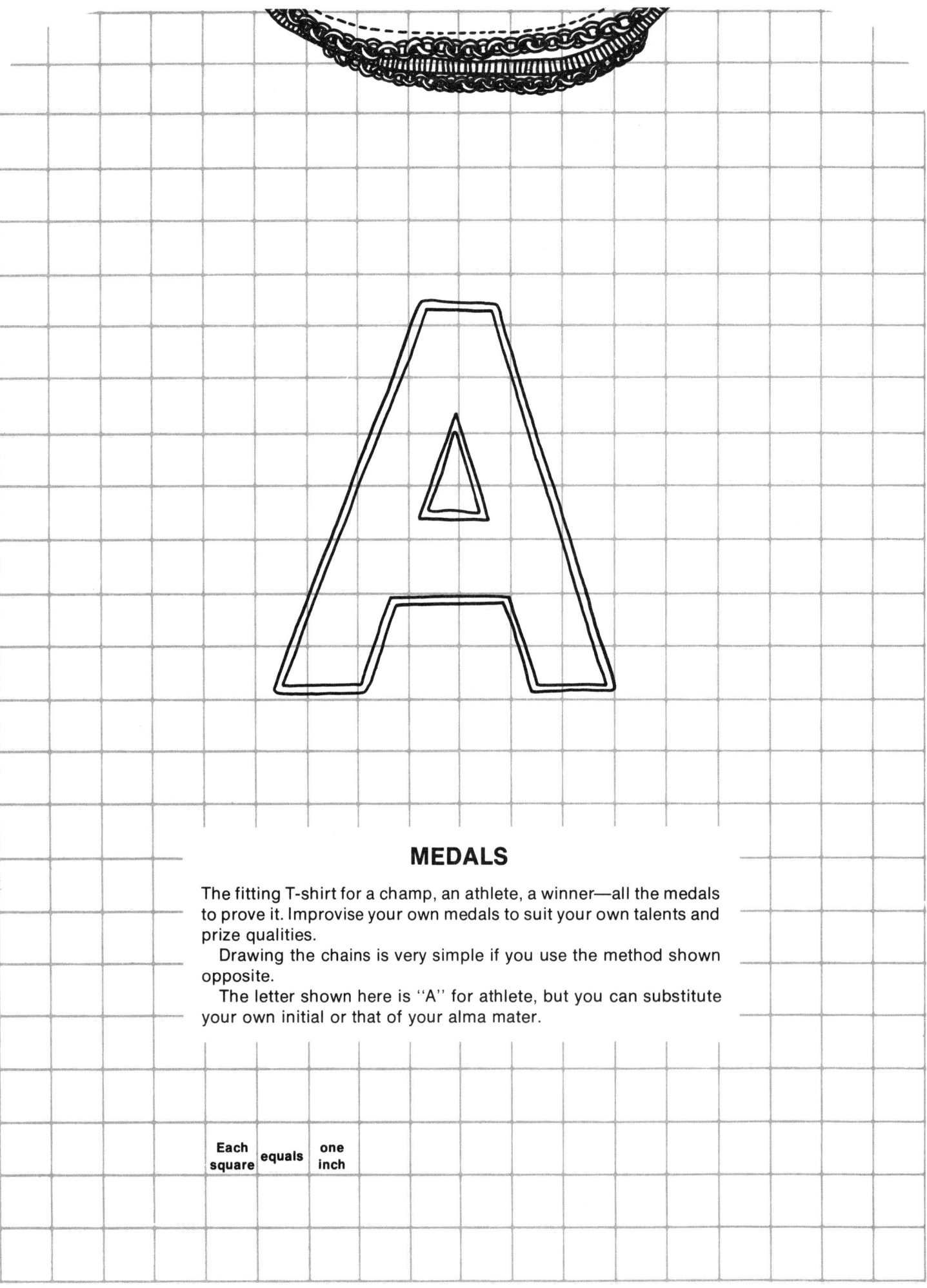

MEDALS

The fitting T-shirt for a champ, an athlete, a winner—all the medals to prove it. Improvise your own medals to suit your own talents and prize qualities.

Drawing the chains is very simple if you use the method shown opposite.

The letter shown here is "A" for athlete, but you can substitute your own initial or that of your alma mater.

Each square	equals	one inch

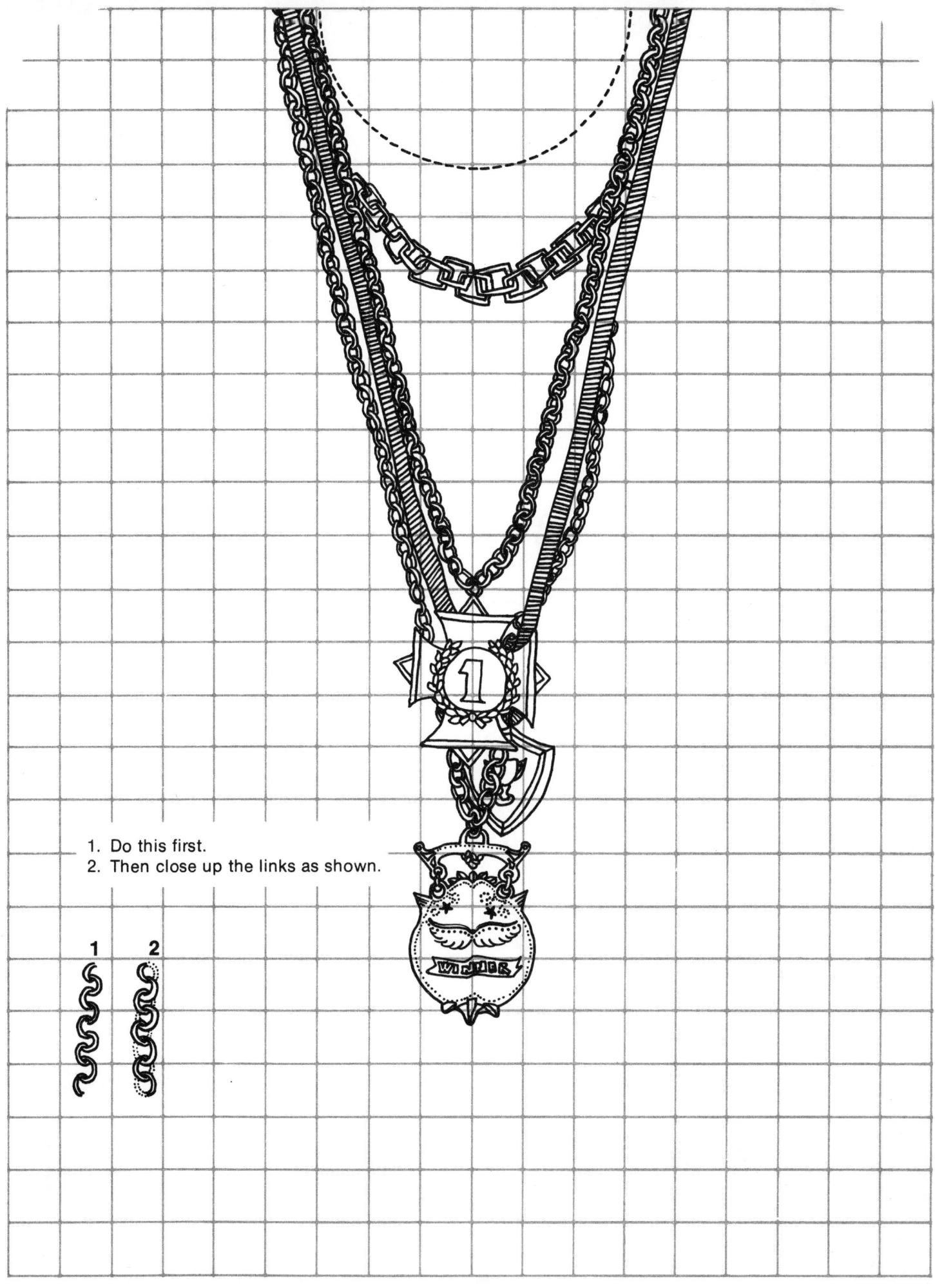

1. Do this first.
2. Then close up the links as shown.

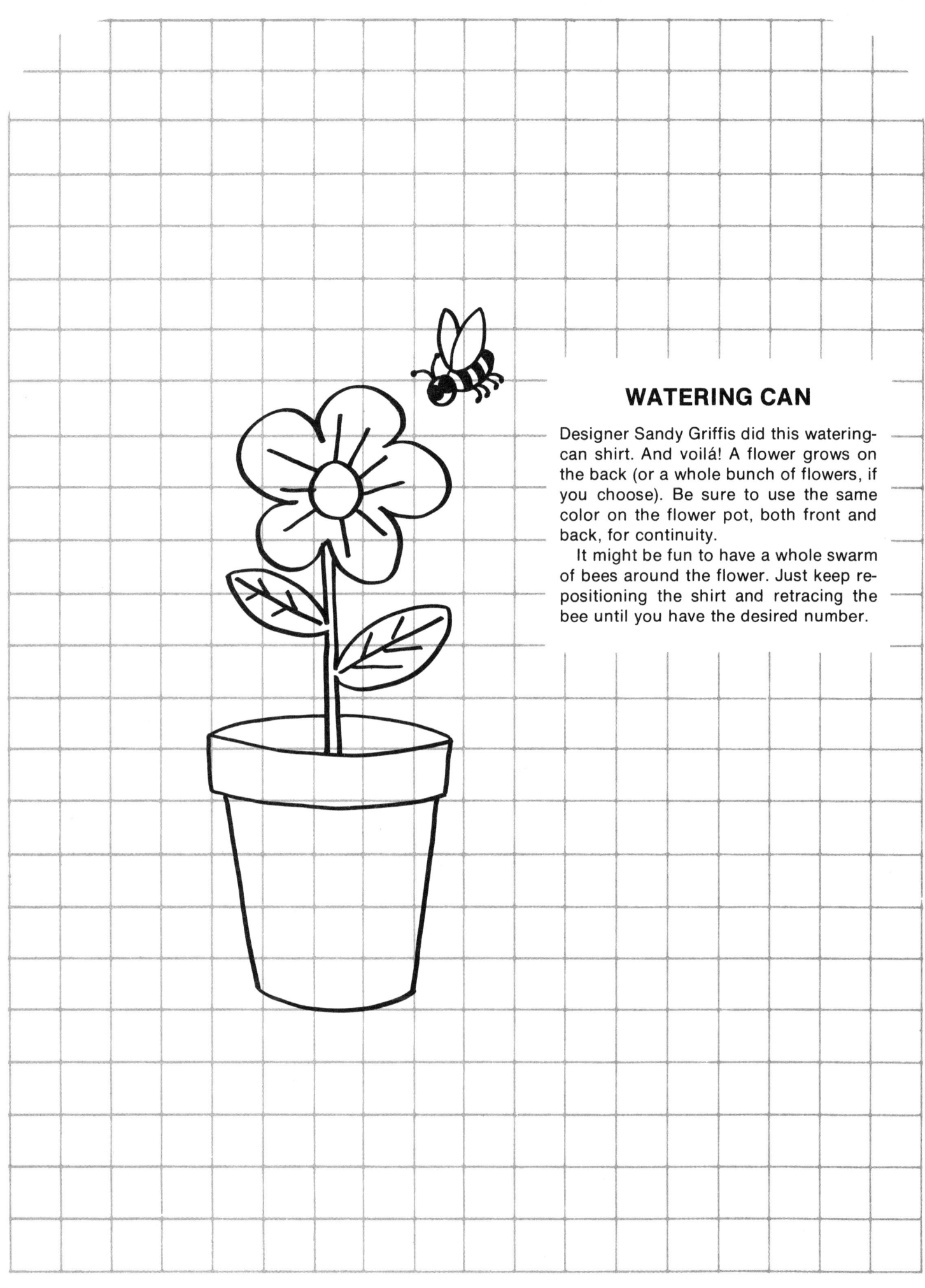

WATERING CAN

Designer Sandy Griffis did this watering-can shirt. And voilá! A flower grows on the back (or a whole bunch of flowers, if you choose). Be sure to use the same color on the flower pot, both front and back, for continuity.

It might be fun to have a whole swarm of bees around the flower. Just keep repositioning the shirt and retracing the bee until you have the desired number.

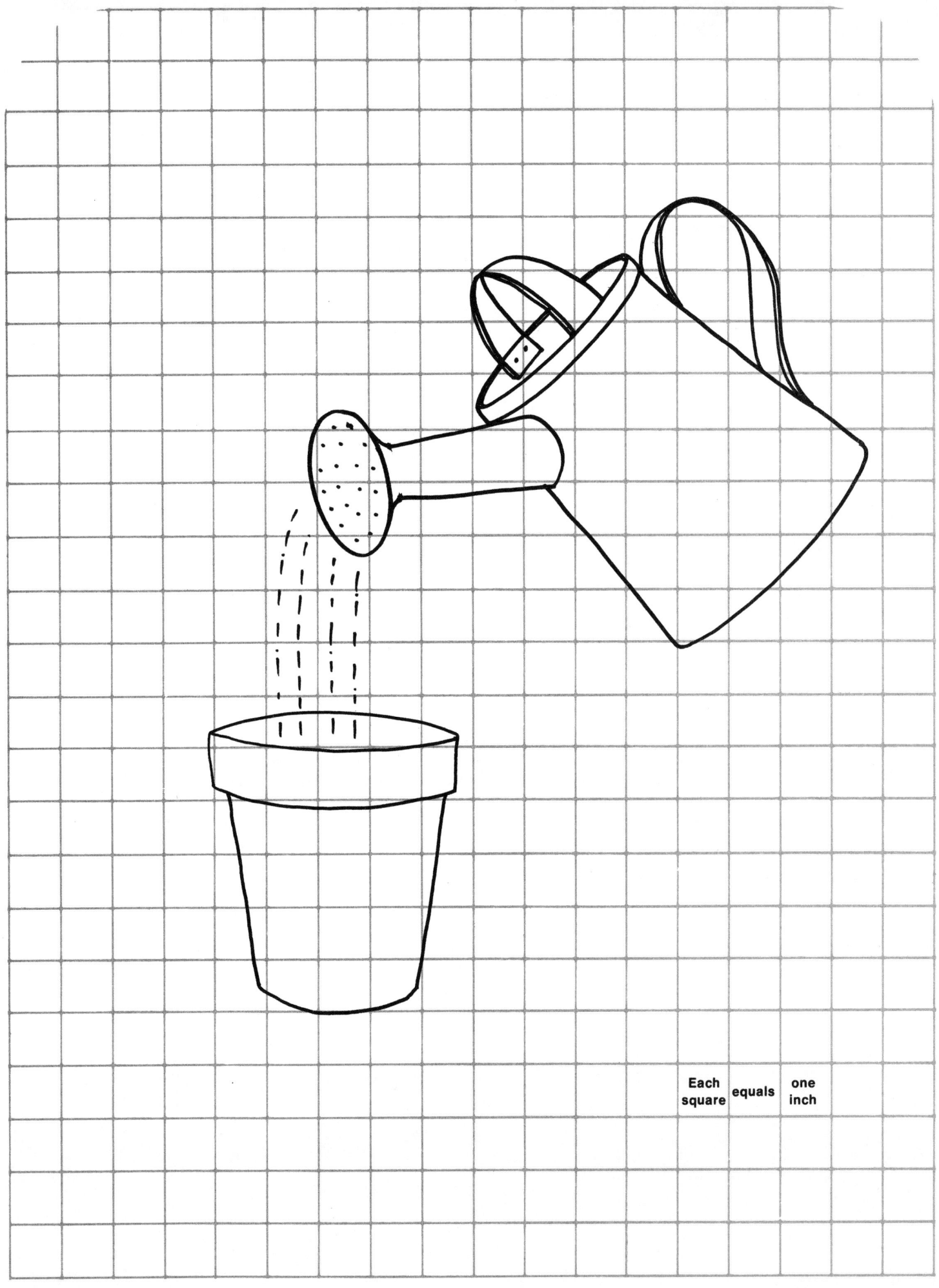

Each square equals one inch

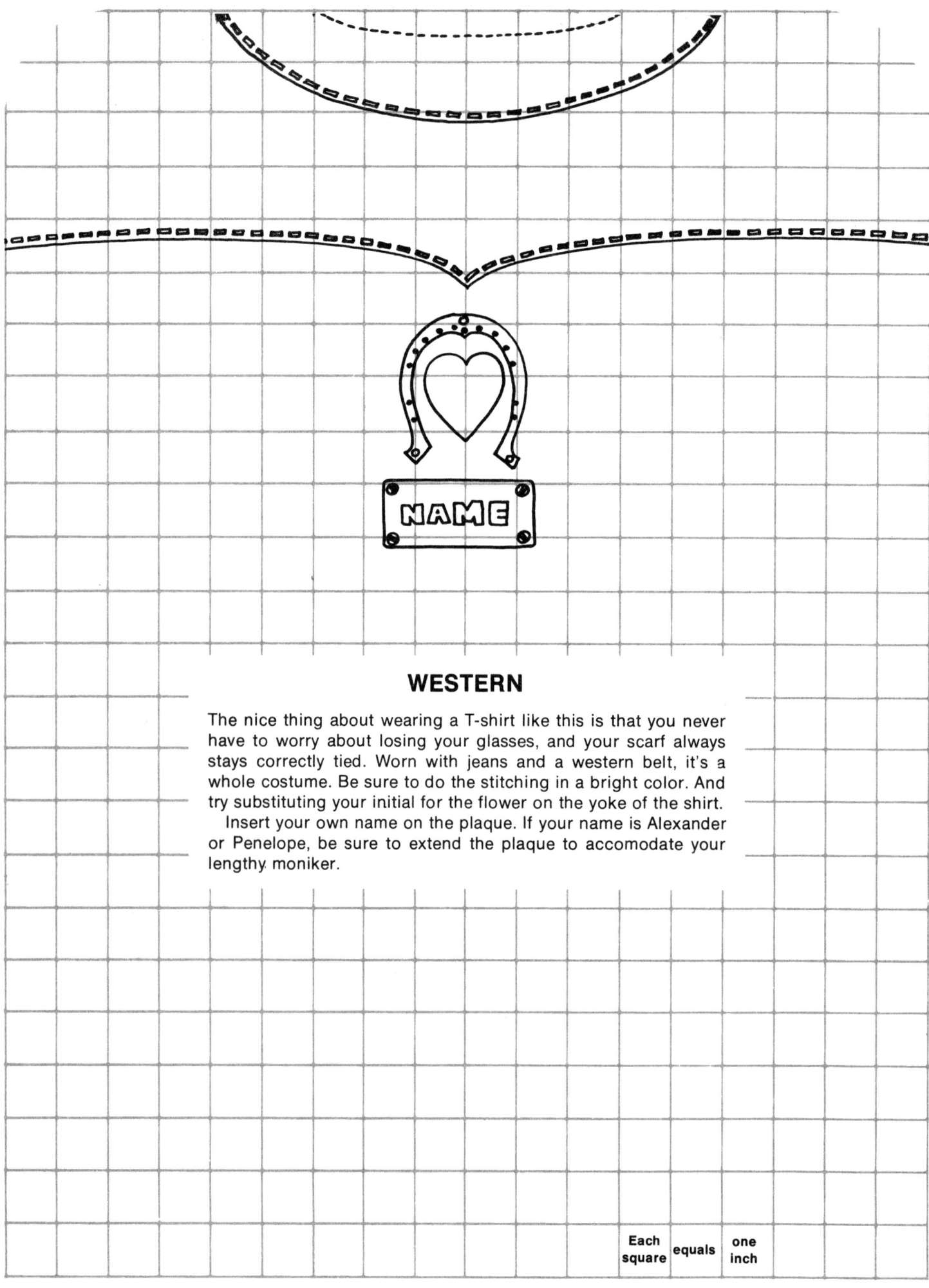

WESTERN

The nice thing about wearing a T-shirt like this is that you never have to worry about losing your glasses, and your scarf always stays correctly tied. Worn with jeans and a western belt, it's a whole costume. Be sure to do the stitching in a bright color. And try substituting your initial for the flower on the yoke of the shirt.

Insert your own name on the plaque. If your name is Alexander or Penelope, be sure to extend the plaque to accomodate your lengthy moniker.

Each square equals one inch

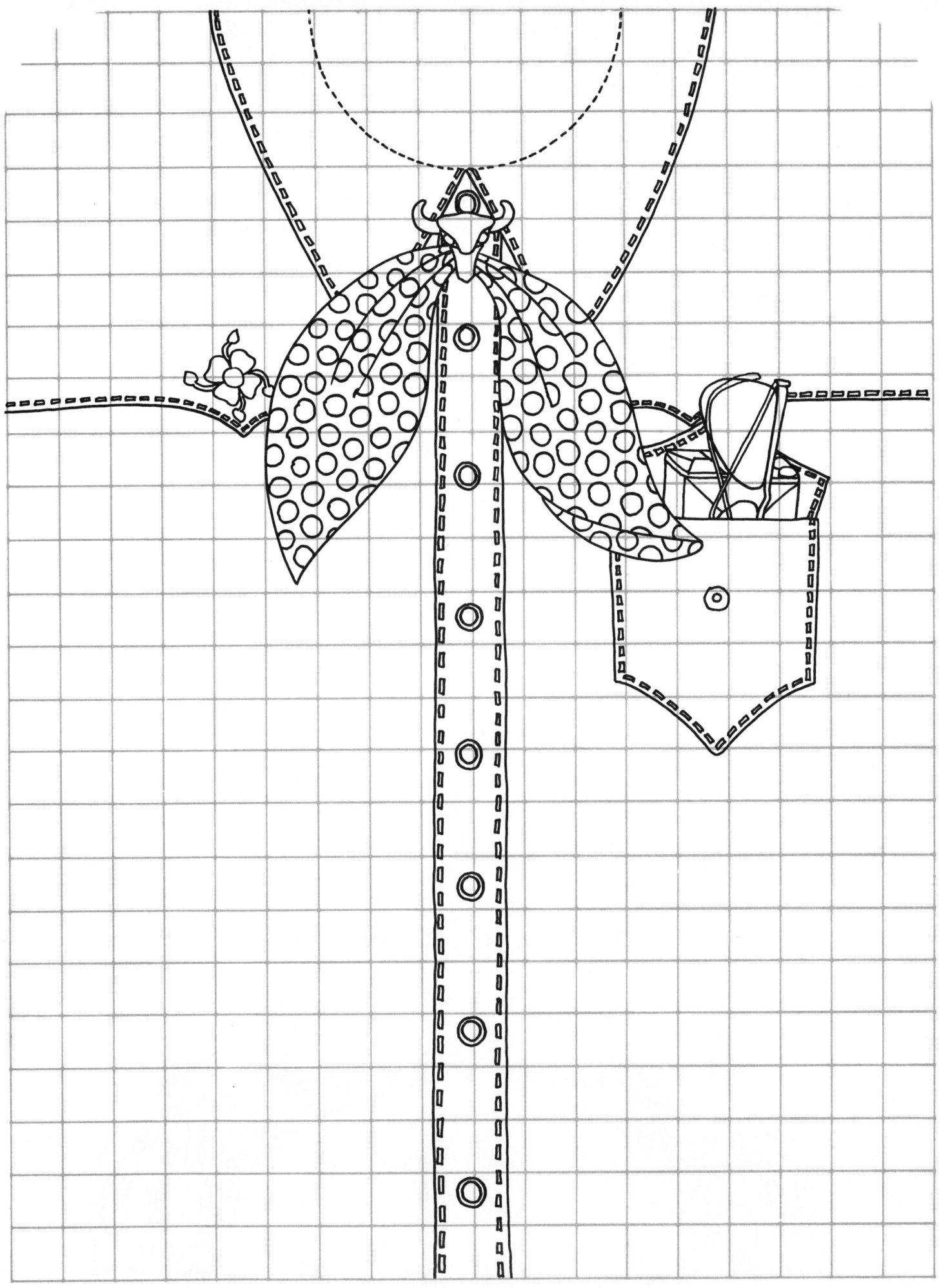

MESSAGE / THOUGHT

This is your chance to speak your mind. There are endless combinations of word/thought messages that you might use; here are just a few:

Front	Back
HI, MY NAME IS LULU	BUT I DON'T GIVE OUT MY PHONE NUMBER.
HAPPY BIRTHDAY	AND MANY MORE
I'M A LEO	BUT I HATE ASTROLOGY
WHAT HAS FOUR WHEELS AND FLIES?	A GARBAGE TRUCK [or use any other riddle]

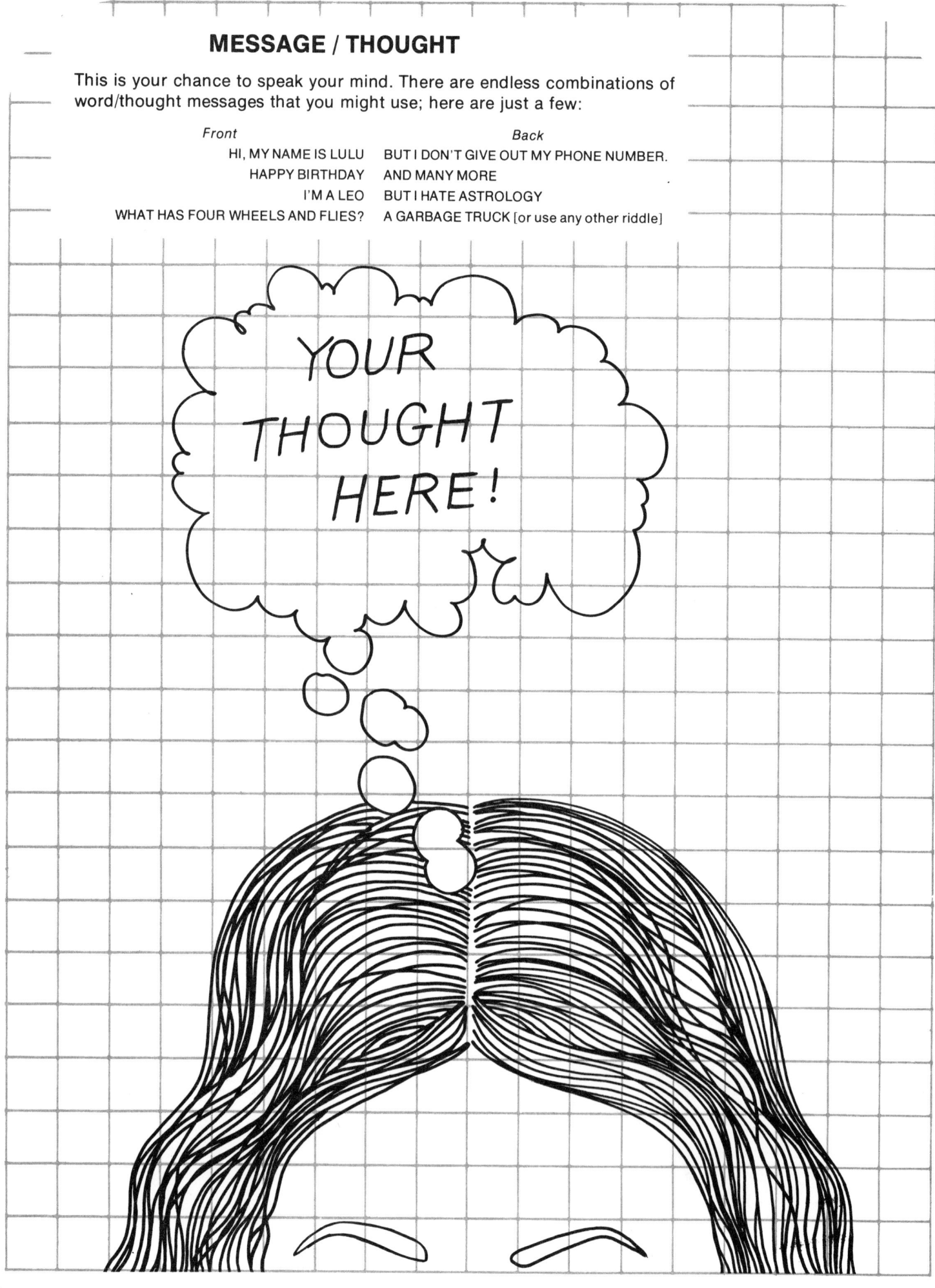

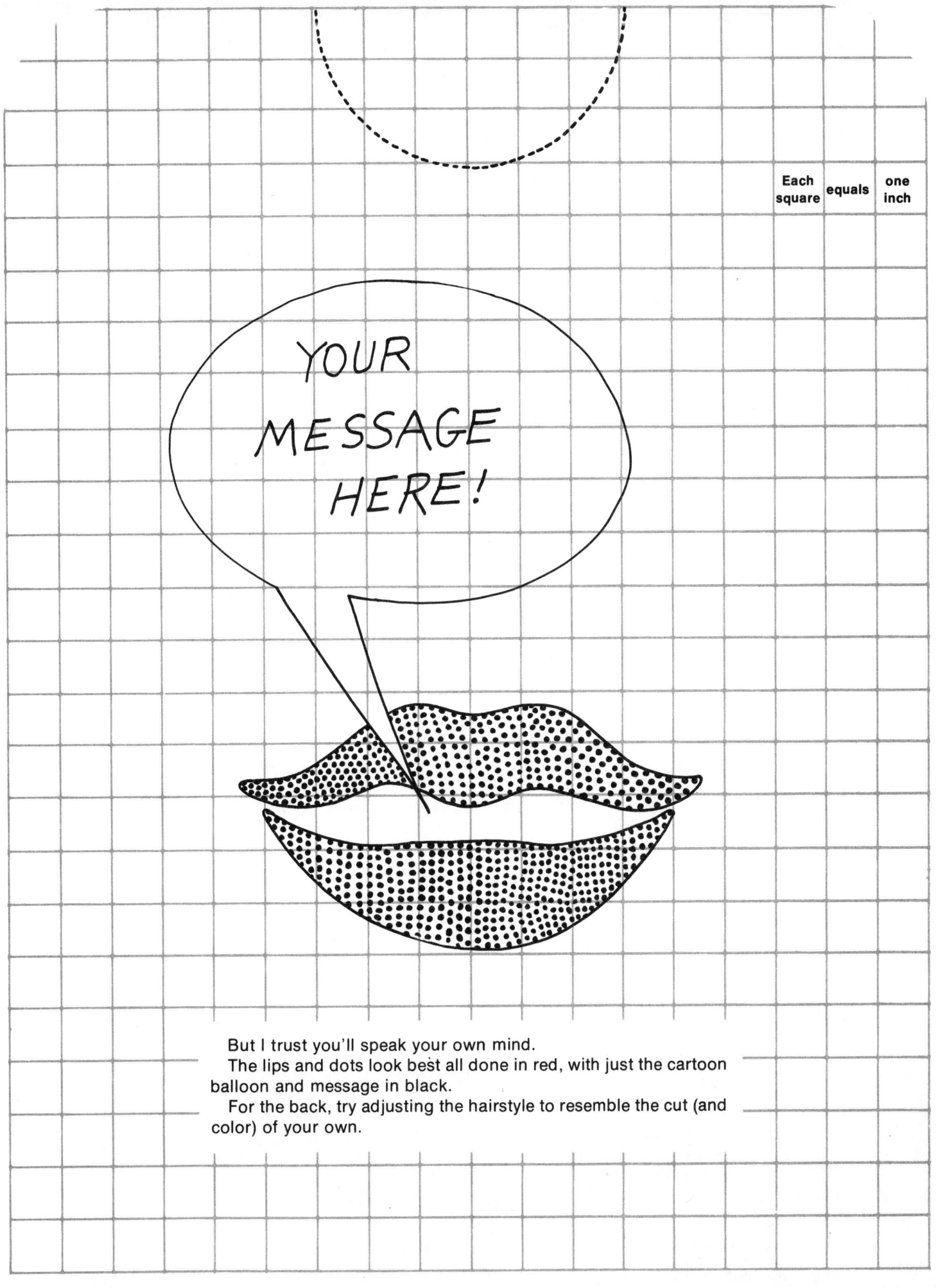

But I trust you'll speak your own mind.

The lips and dots look best all done in red, with just the cartoon balloon and message in black.

For the back, try adjusting the hairstyle to resemble the cut (and color) of your own.

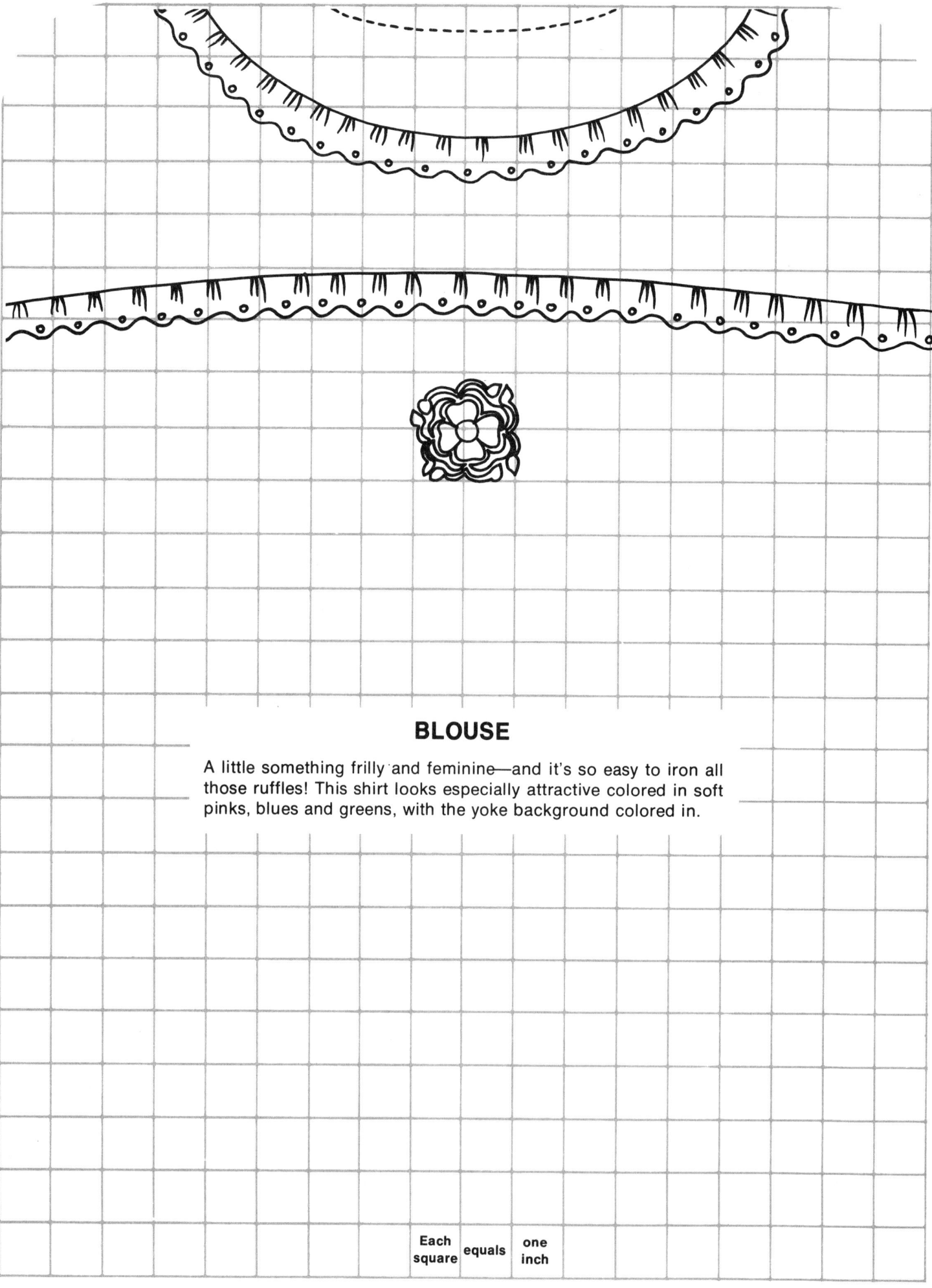

BLOUSE

A little something frilly and feminine—and it's so easy to iron all those ruffles! This shirt looks especially attractive colored in soft pinks, blues and greens, with the yoke background colored in.

Each square equals one inch

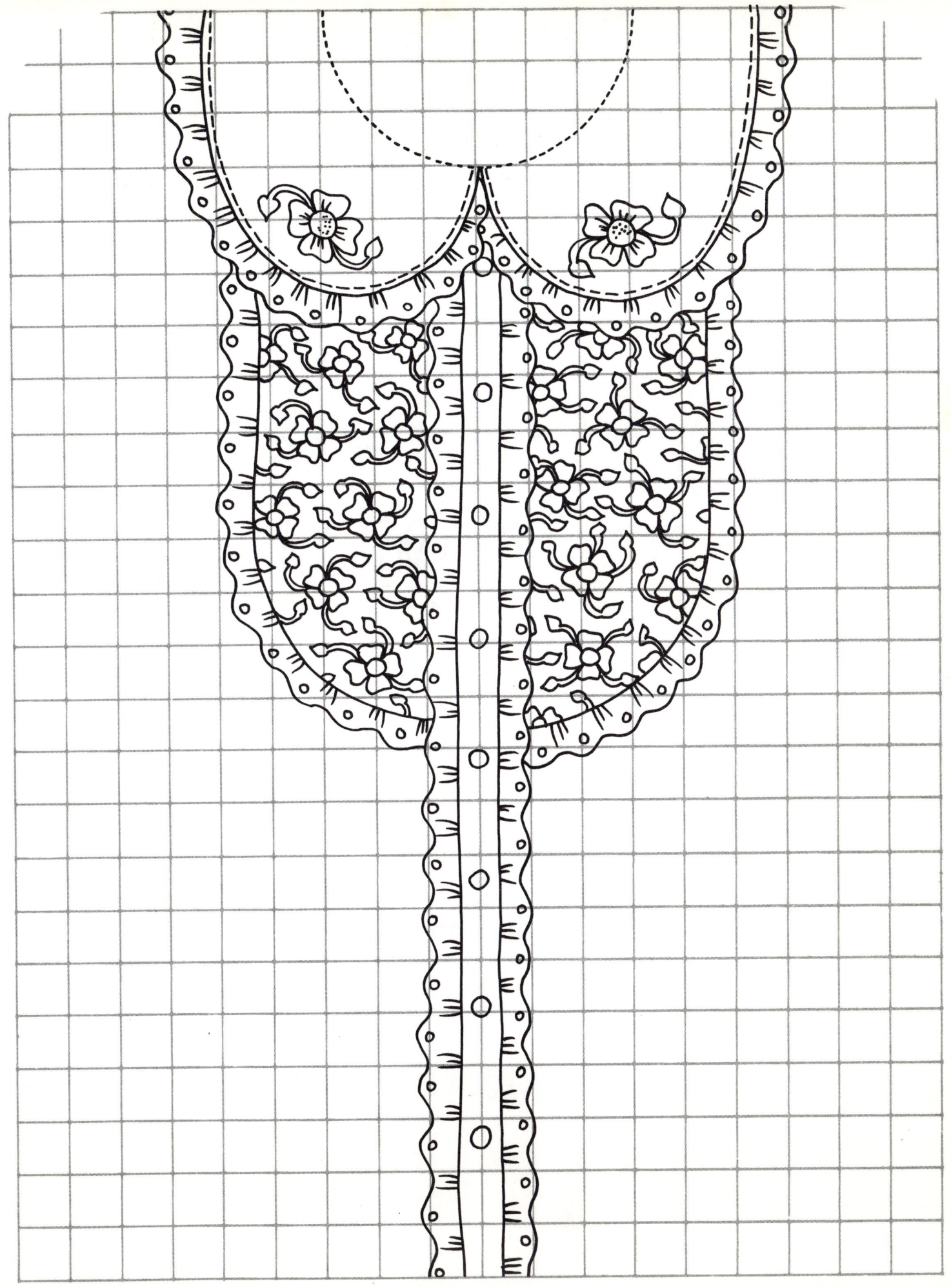

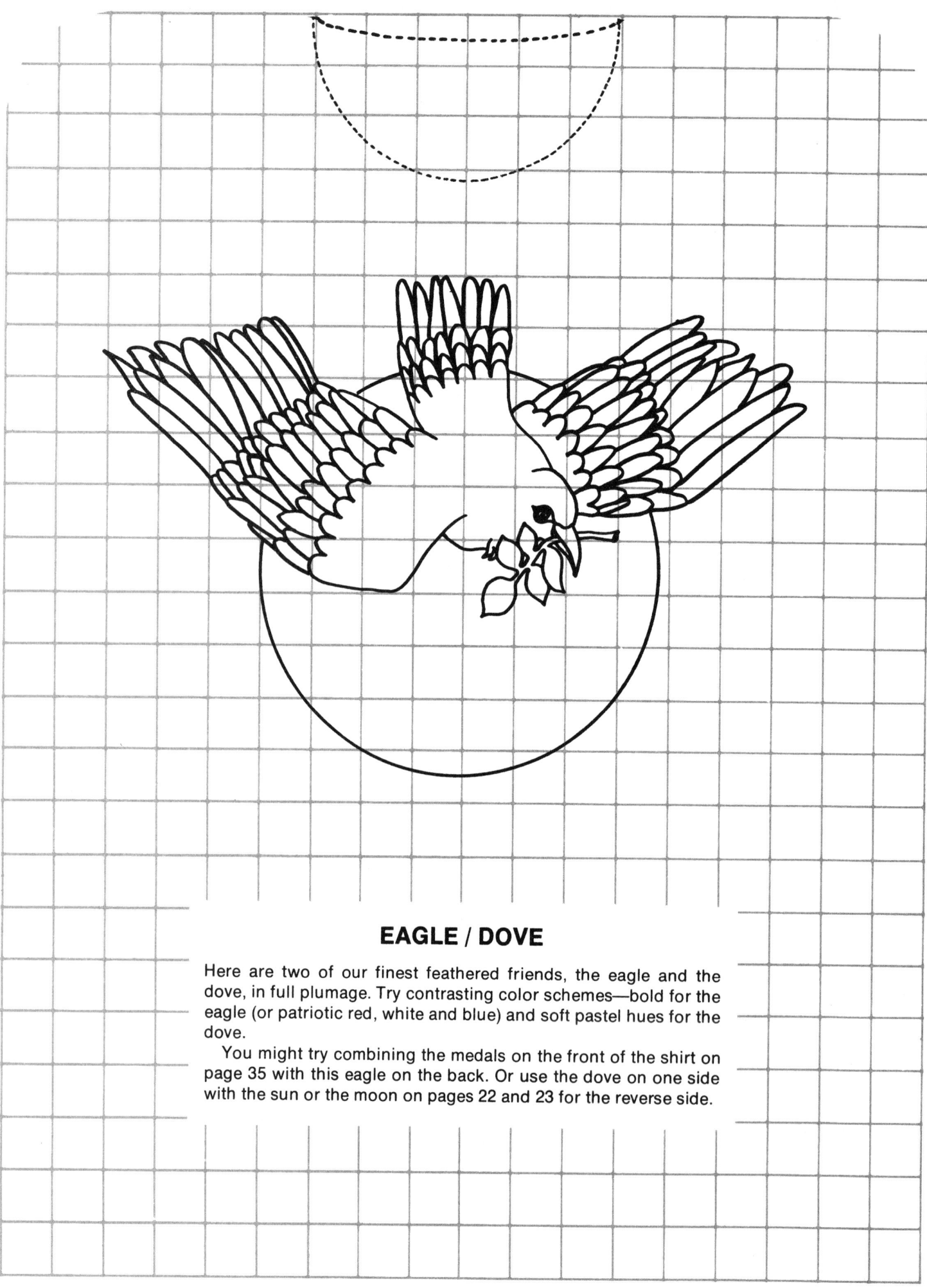

EAGLE / DOVE

Here are two of our finest feathered friends, the eagle and the dove, in full plumage. Try contrasting color schemes—bold for the eagle (or patriotic red, white and blue) and soft pastel hues for the dove.

You might try combining the medals on the front of the shirt on page 35 with this eagle on the back. Or use the dove on one side with the sun or the moon on pages 22 and 23 for the reverse side.

Each square equals one inch

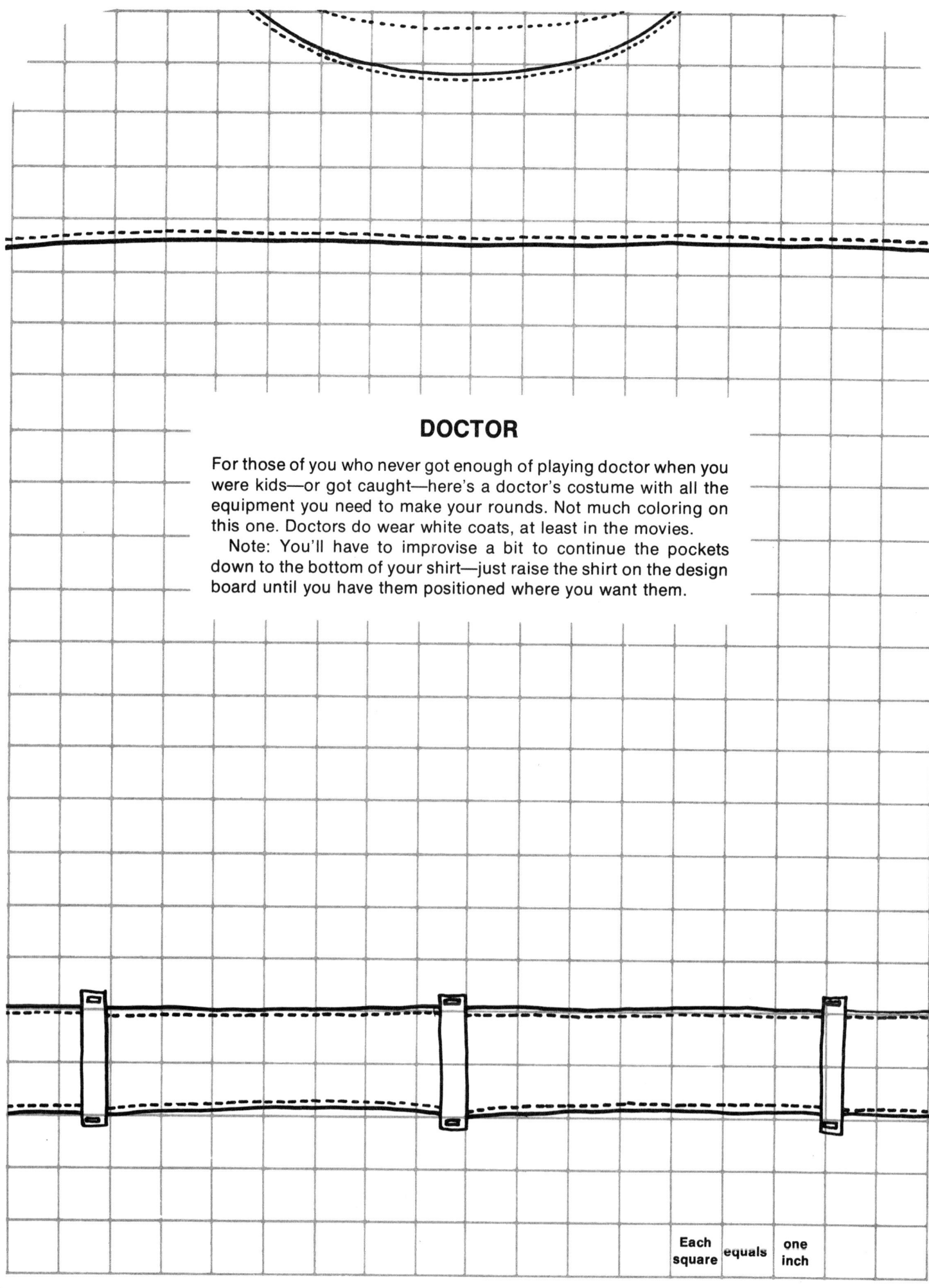

DOCTOR

For those of you who never got enough of playing doctor when you were kids—or got caught—here's a doctor's costume with all the equipment you need to make your rounds. Not much coloring on this one. Doctors do wear white coats, at least in the movies.

Note: You'll have to improvise a bit to continue the pockets down to the bottom of your shirt—just raise the shirt on the design board until you have them positioned where you want them.

Each square equals one inch

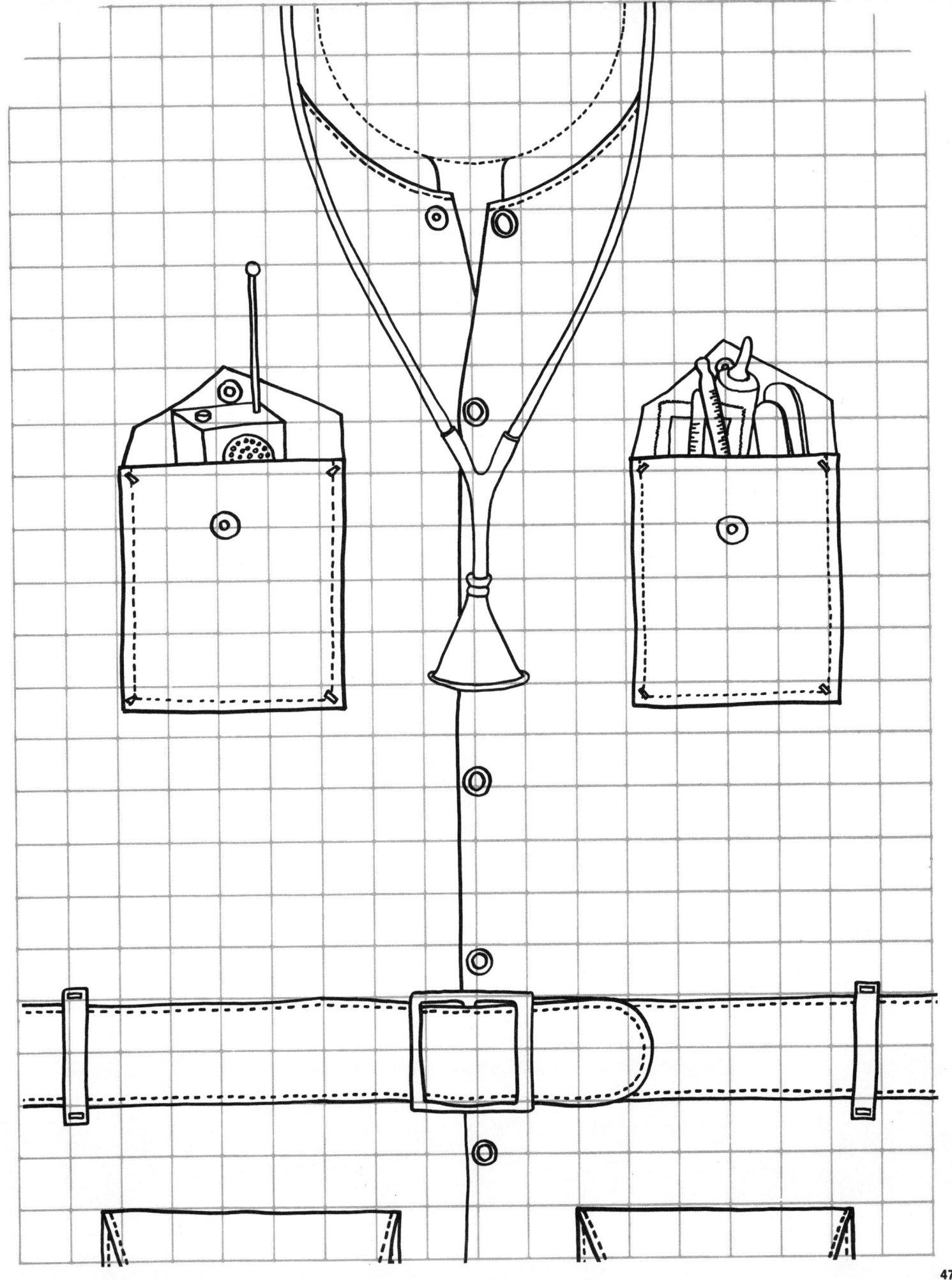

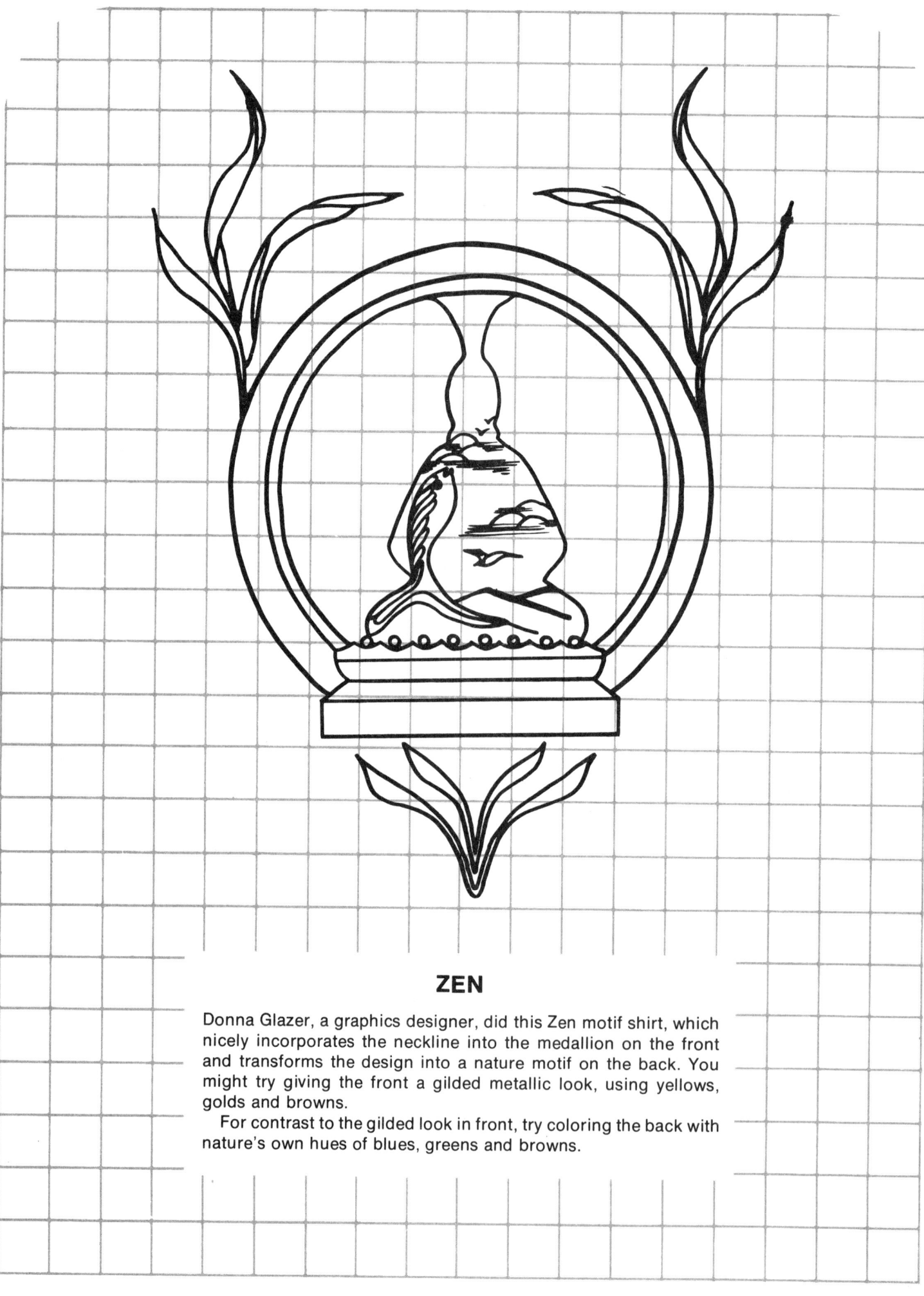

ZEN

Donna Glazer, a graphics designer, did this Zen motif shirt, which nicely incorporates the neckline into the medallion on the front and transforms the design into a nature motif on the back. You might try giving the front a gilded metallic look, using yellows, golds and browns.

For contrast to the gilded look in front, try coloring the back with nature's own hues of blues, greens and browns.

Each square equals one inch

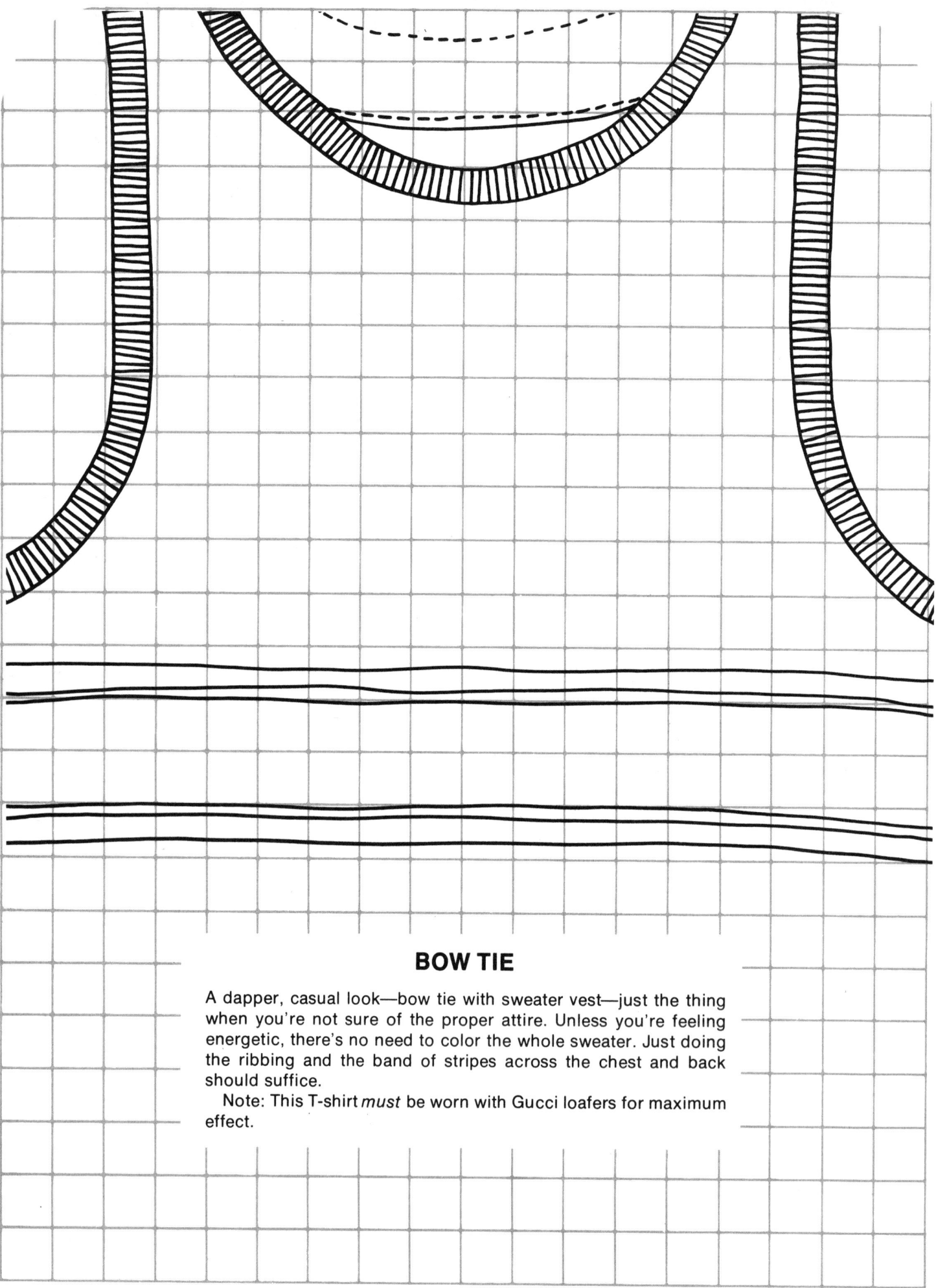

BOW TIE

A dapper, casual look—bow tie with sweater vest—just the thing when you're not sure of the proper attire. Unless you're feeling energetic, there's no need to color the whole sweater. Just doing the ribbing and the band of stripes across the chest and back should suffice.

Note: This T-shirt *must* be worn with Gucci loafers for maximum effect.

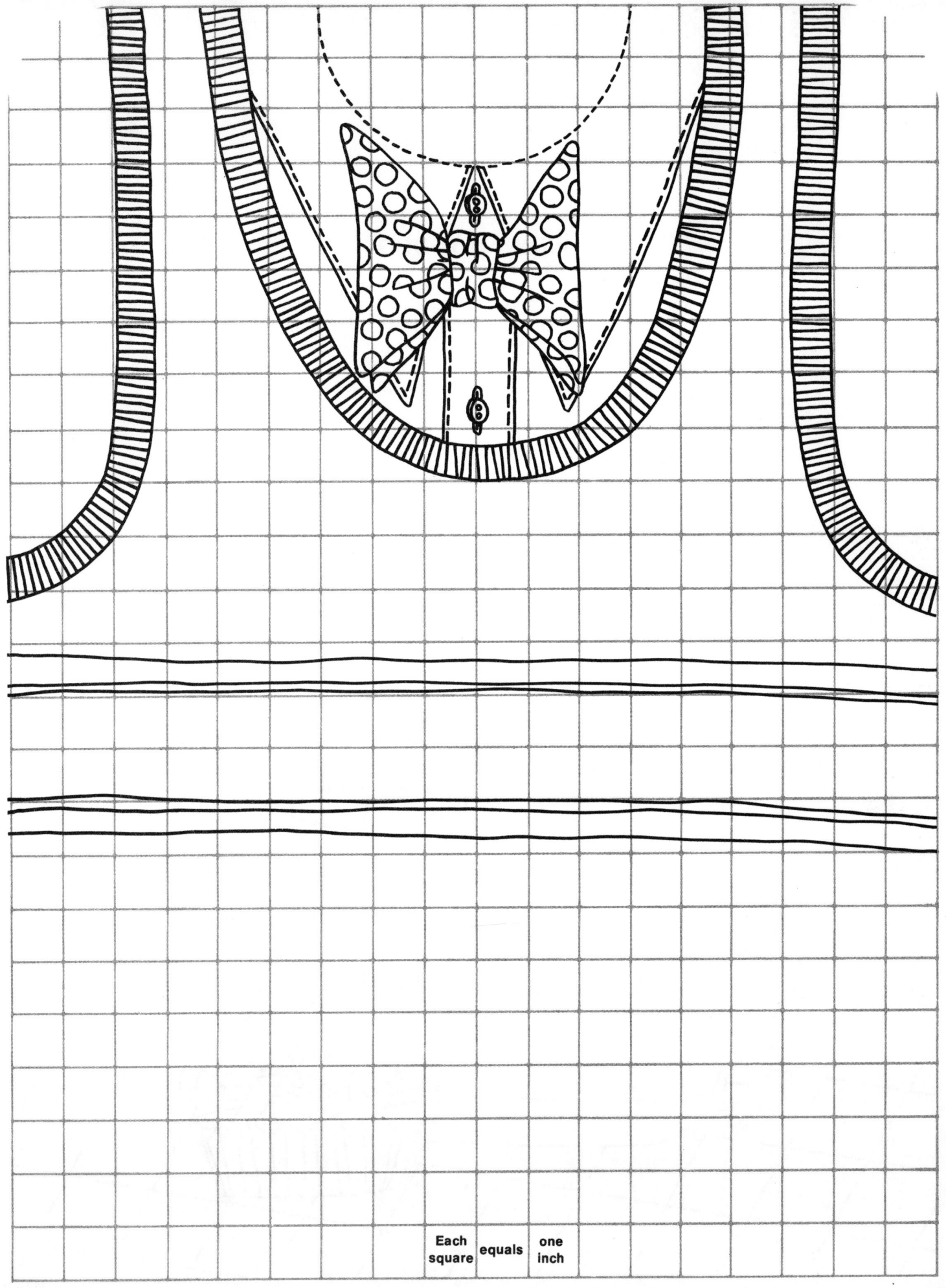

Each square equals one inch

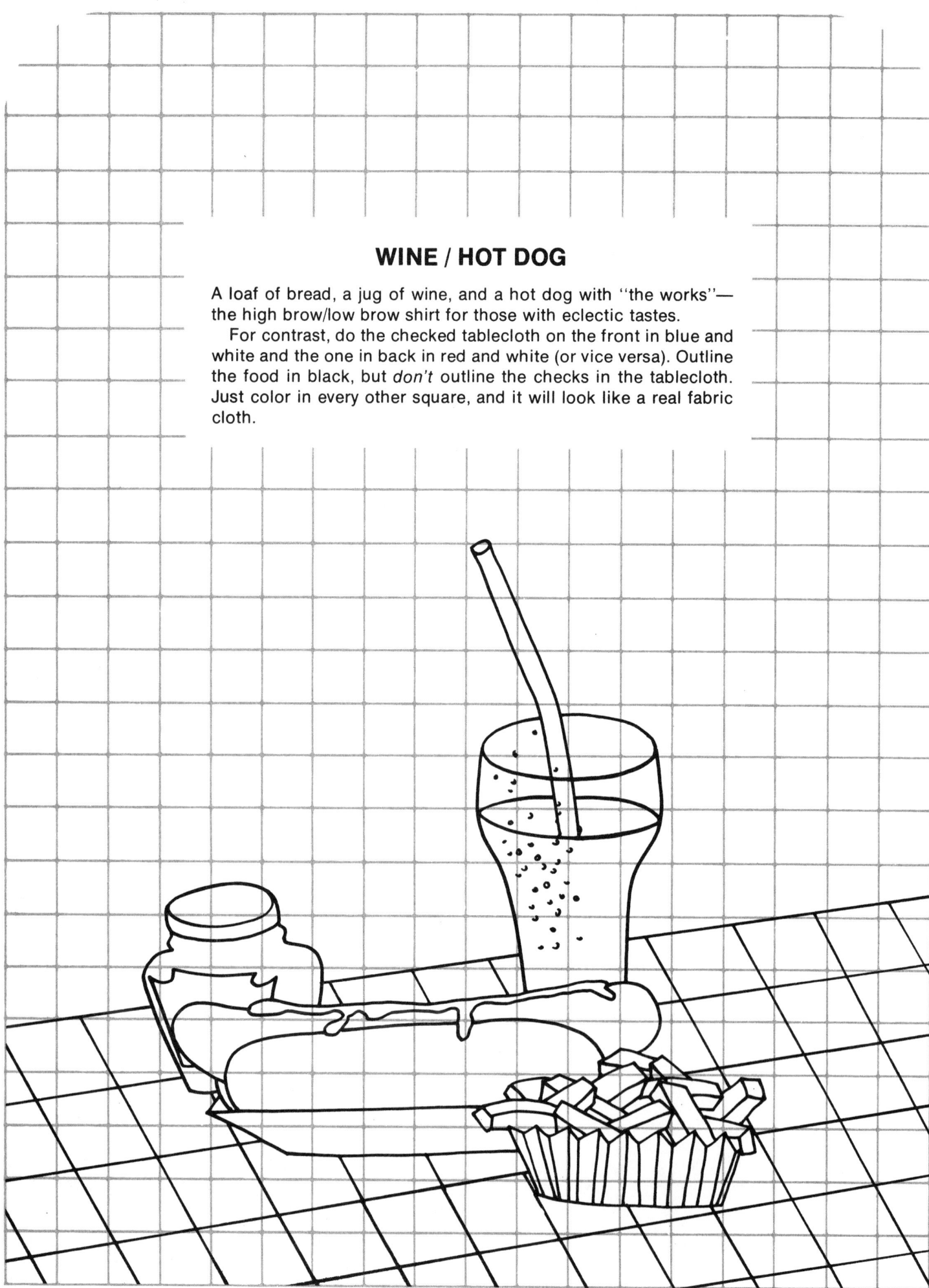

WINE / HOT DOG

A loaf of bread, a jug of wine, and a hot dog with "the works"—the high brow/low brow shirt for those with eclectic tastes.

For contrast, do the checked tablecloth on the front in blue and white and the one in back in red and white (or vice versa). Outline the food in black, but *don't* outline the checks in the tablecloth. Just color in every other square, and it will look like a real fabric cloth.

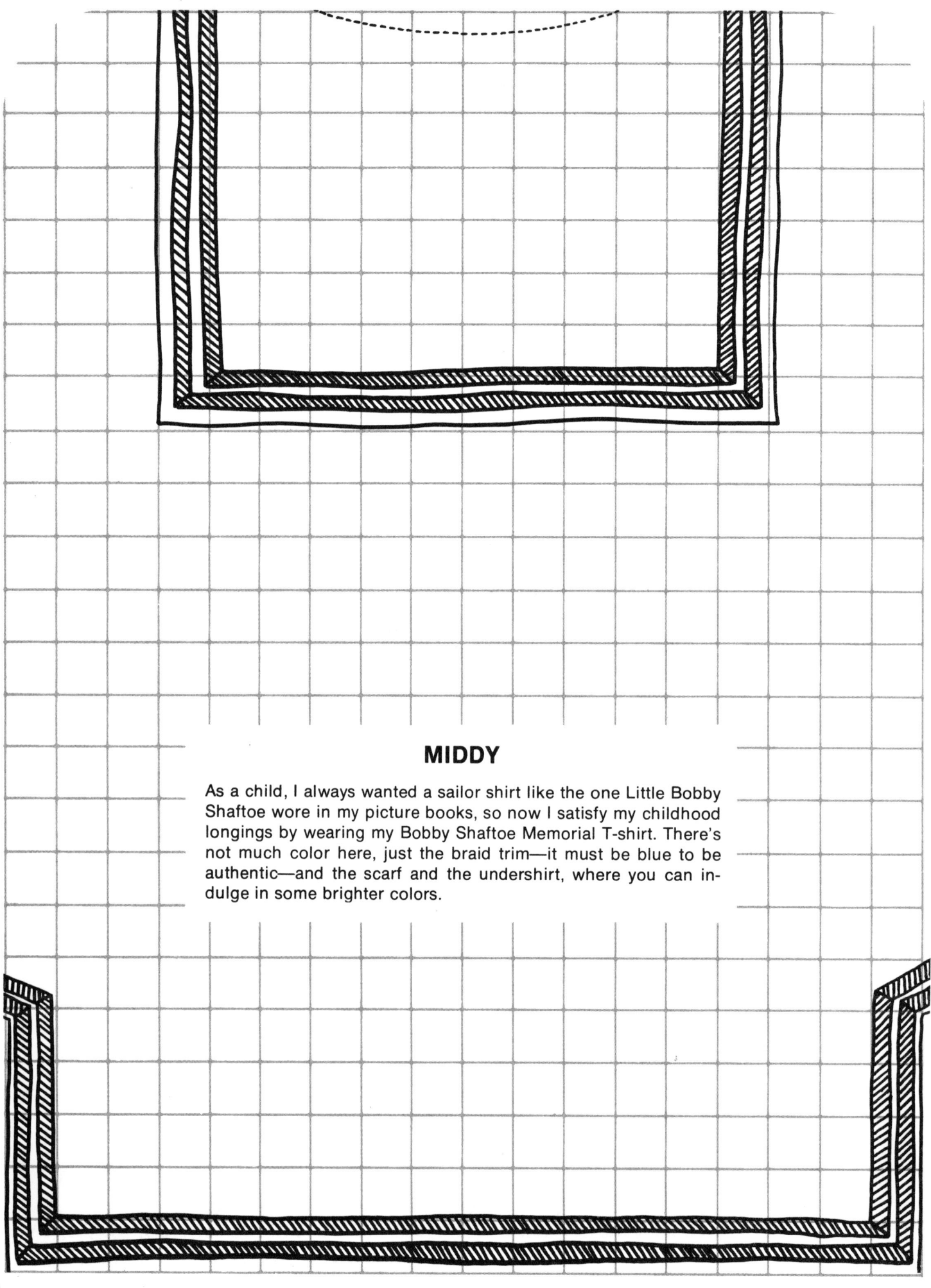

MIDDY

As a child, I always wanted a sailor shirt like the one Little Bobby Shaftoe wore in my picture books, so now I satisfy my childhood longings by wearing my Bobby Shaftoe Memorial T-shirt. There's not much color here, just the braid trim—it must be blue to be authentic—and the scarf and the undershirt, where you can indulge in some brighter colors.

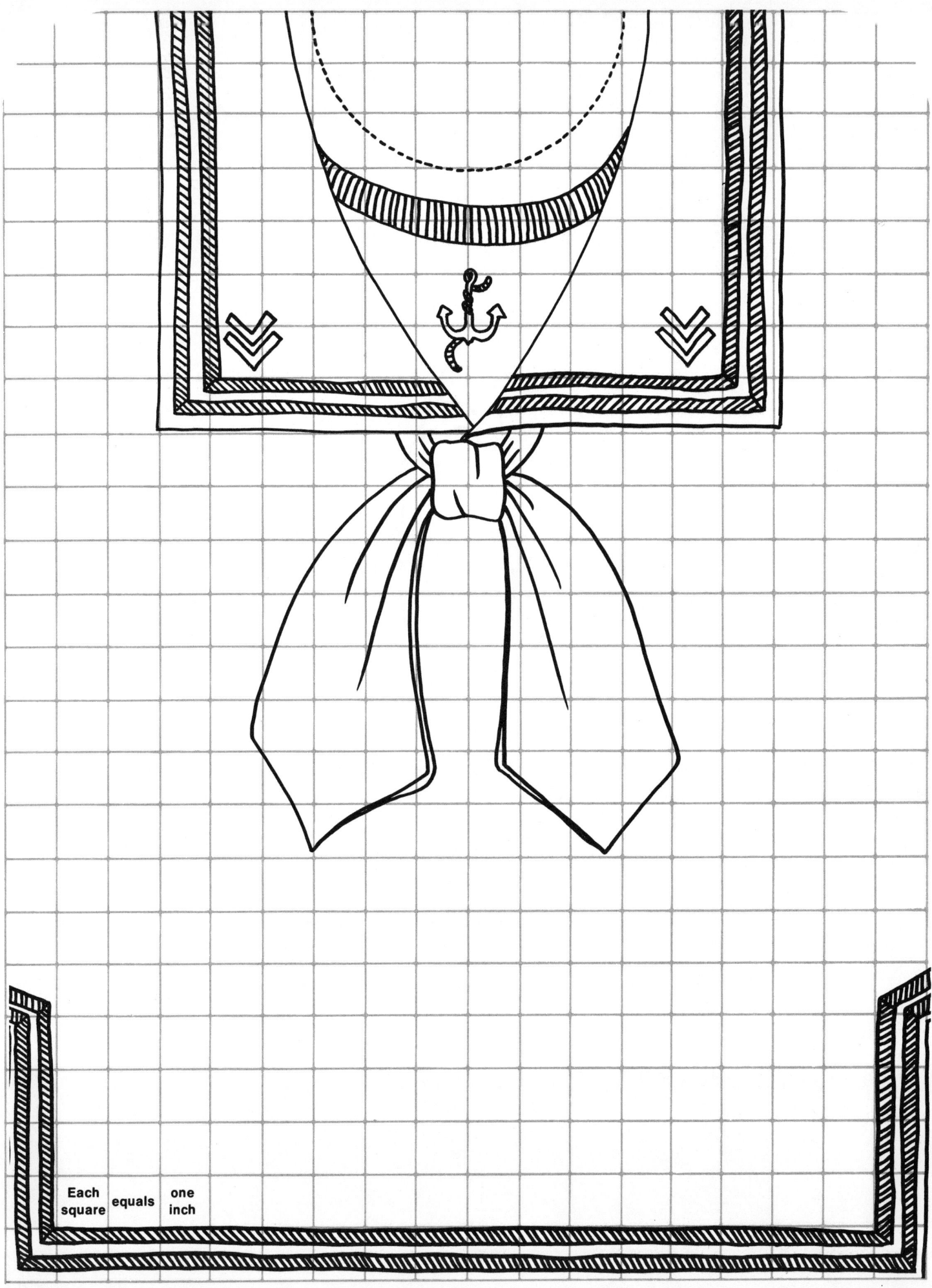

Each square equals one inch

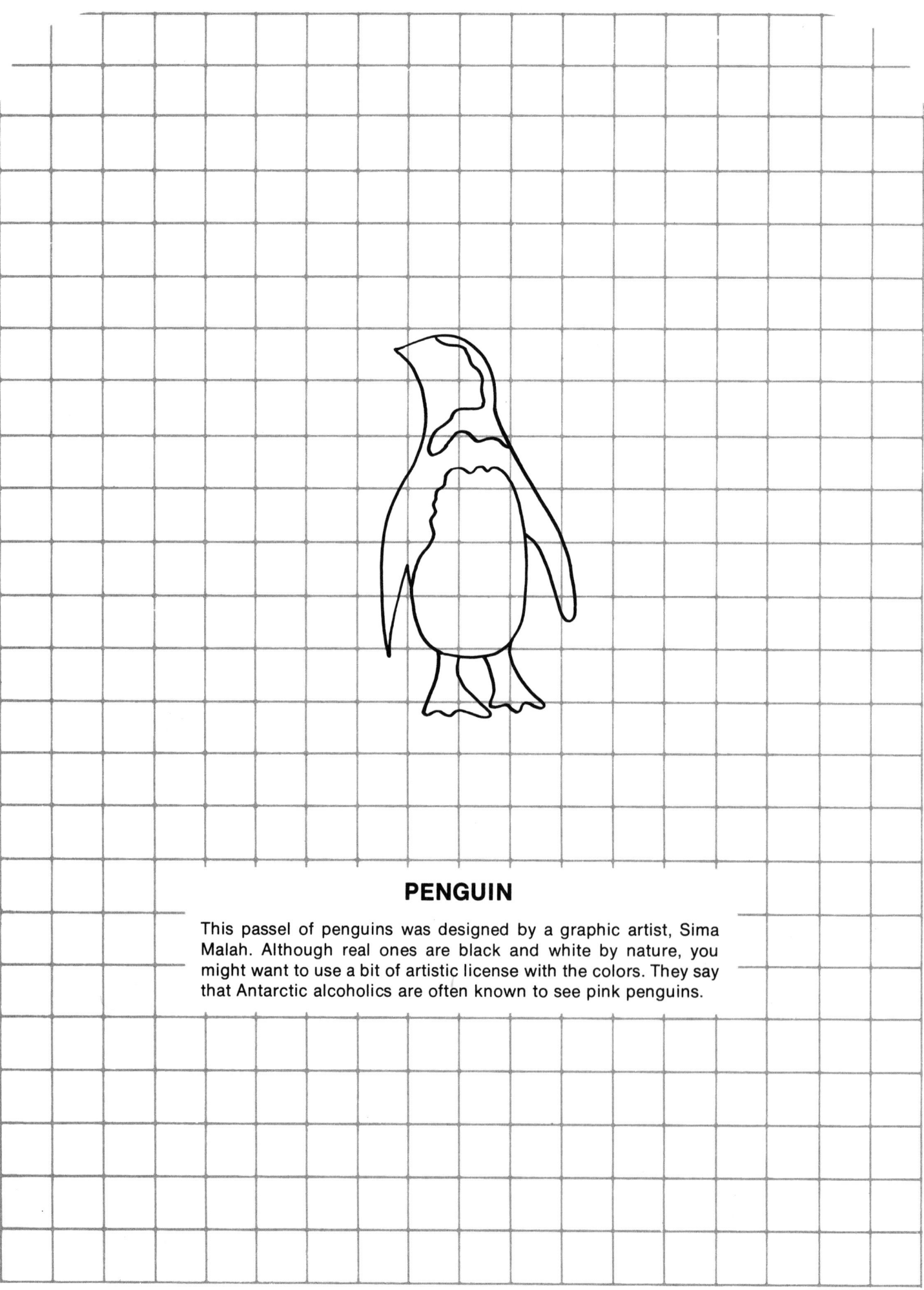

PENGUIN

This passel of penguins was designed by a graphic artist, Sima Malah. Although real ones are black and white by nature, you might want to use a bit of artistic license with the colors. They say that Antarctic alcoholics are often known to see pink penguins.

Each square equals one inch

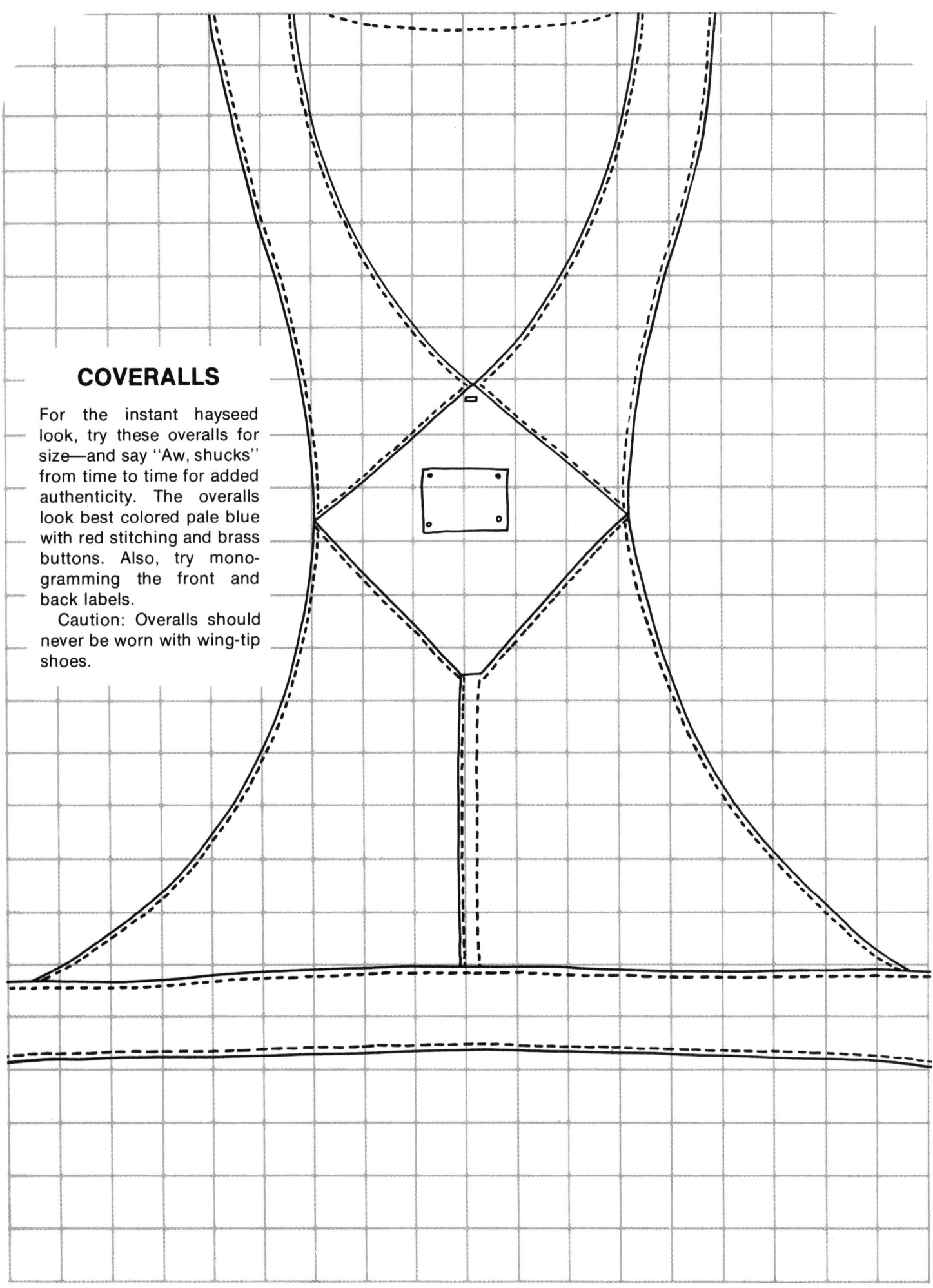

COVERALLS

For the instant hayseed look, try these overalls for size—and say "Aw, shucks" from time to time for added authenticity. The overalls look best colored pale blue with red stitching and brass buttons. Also, try monogramming the front and back labels.

Caution: Overalls should never be worn with wing-tip shoes.

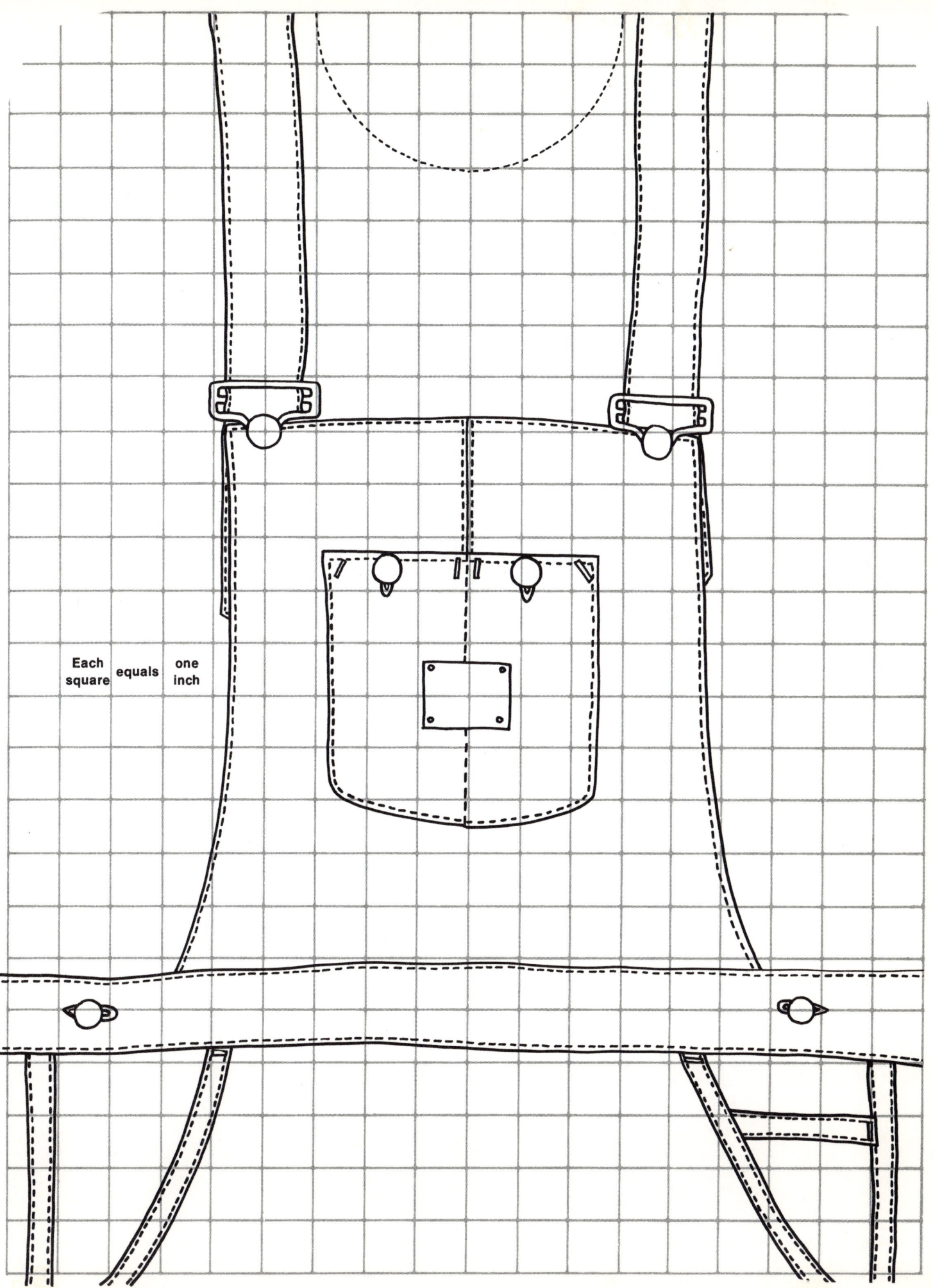

Each square equals one inch

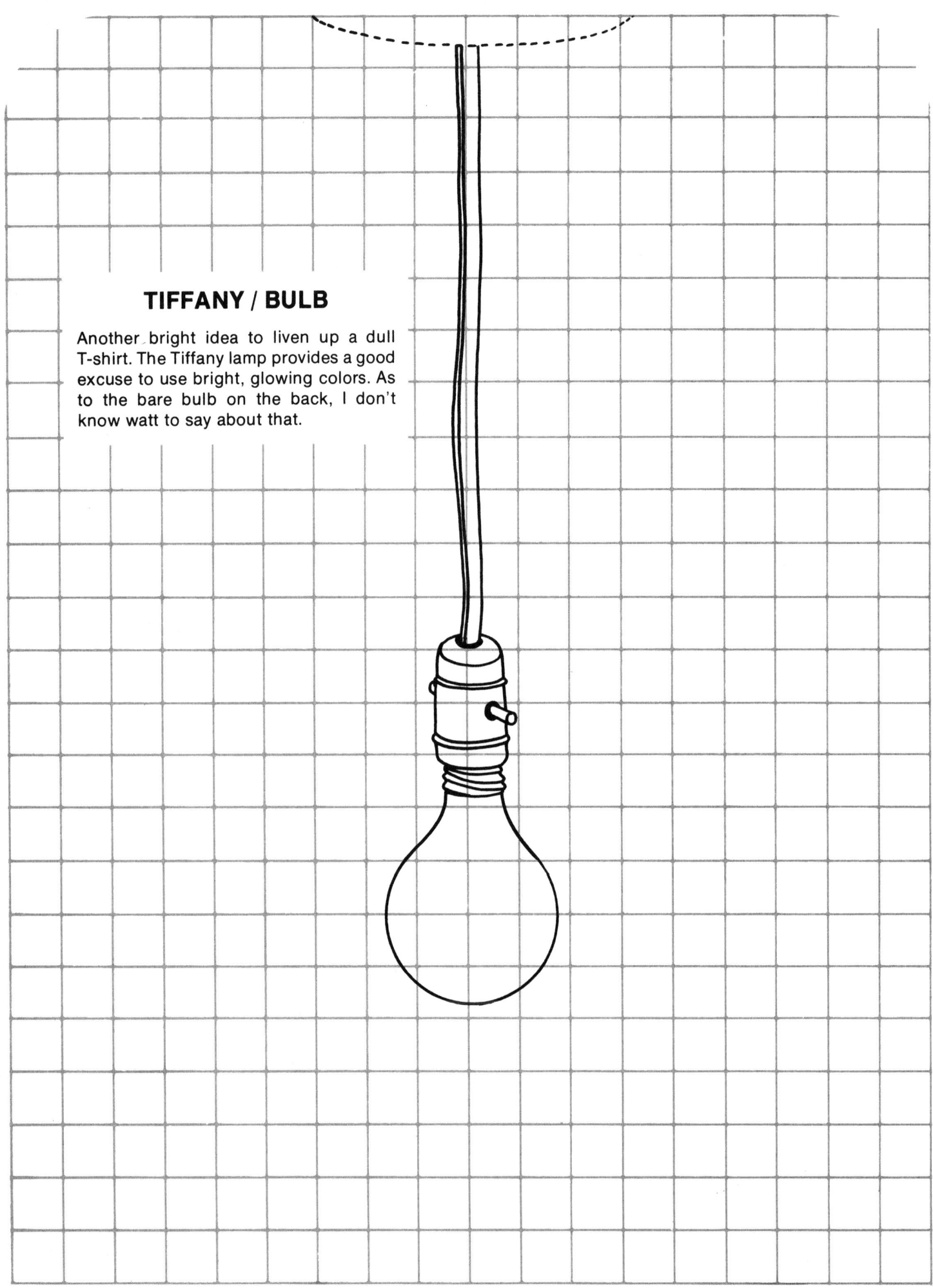

TIFFANY / BULB

Another bright idea to liven up a dull T-shirt. The Tiffany lamp provides a good excuse to use bright, glowing colors. As to the bare bulb on the back, I don't know watt to say about that.

Each square equals one inch

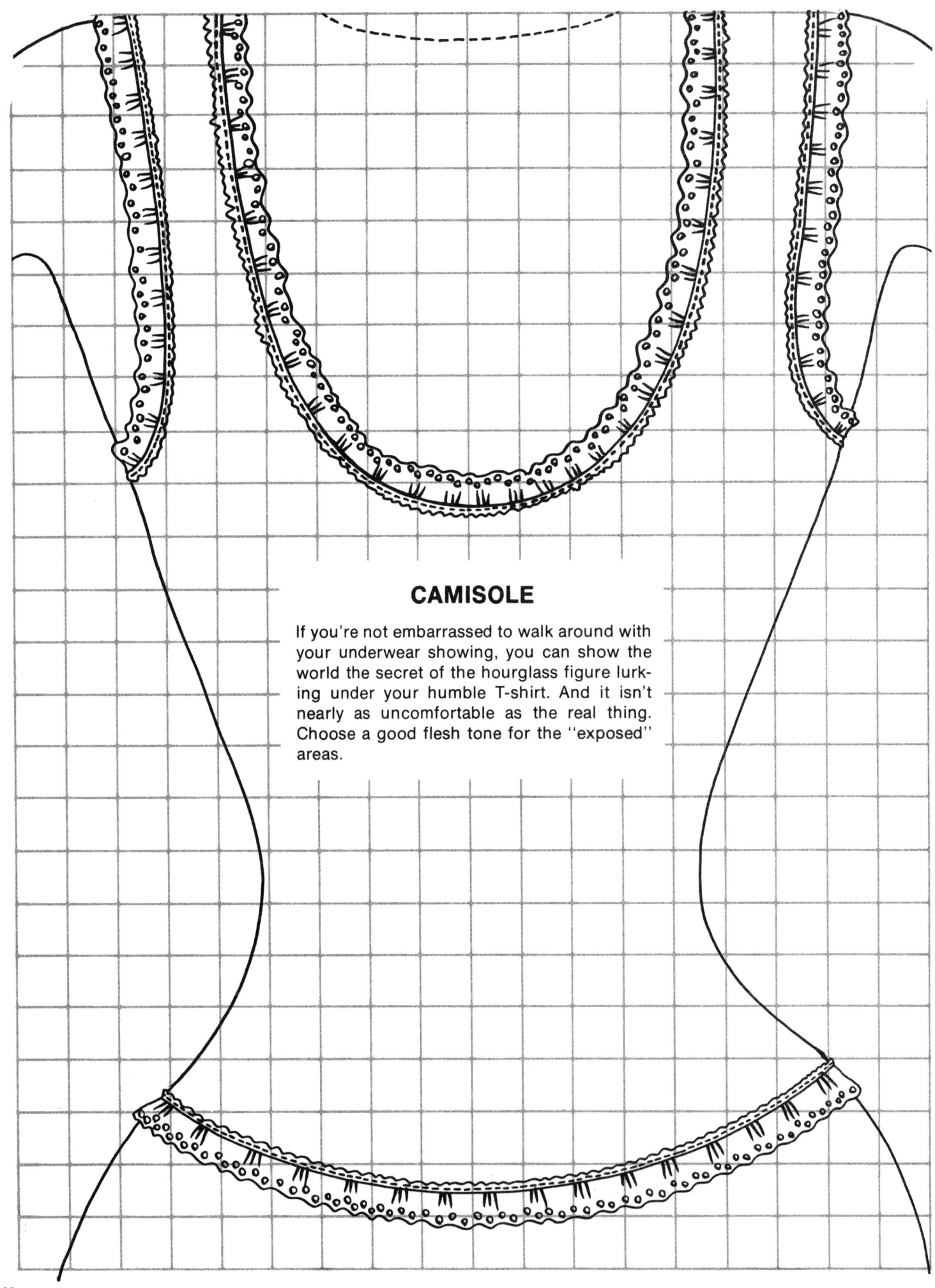

CAMISOLE

If you're not embarrassed to walk around with your underwear showing, you can show the world the secret of the hourglass figure lurking under your humble T-shirt. And it isn't nearly as uncomfortable as the real thing. Choose a good flesh tone for the "exposed" areas.

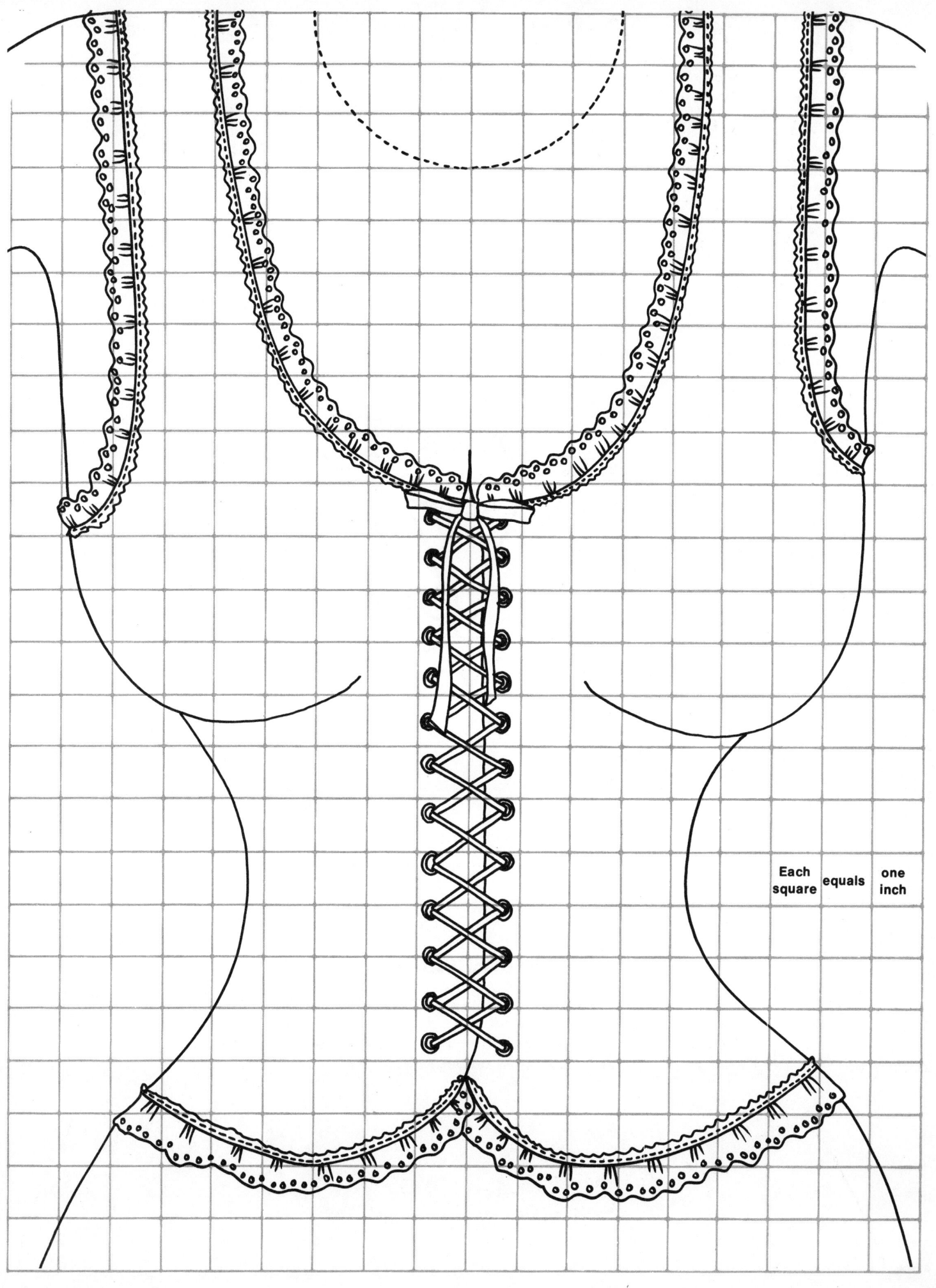

Each square equals one inch

63

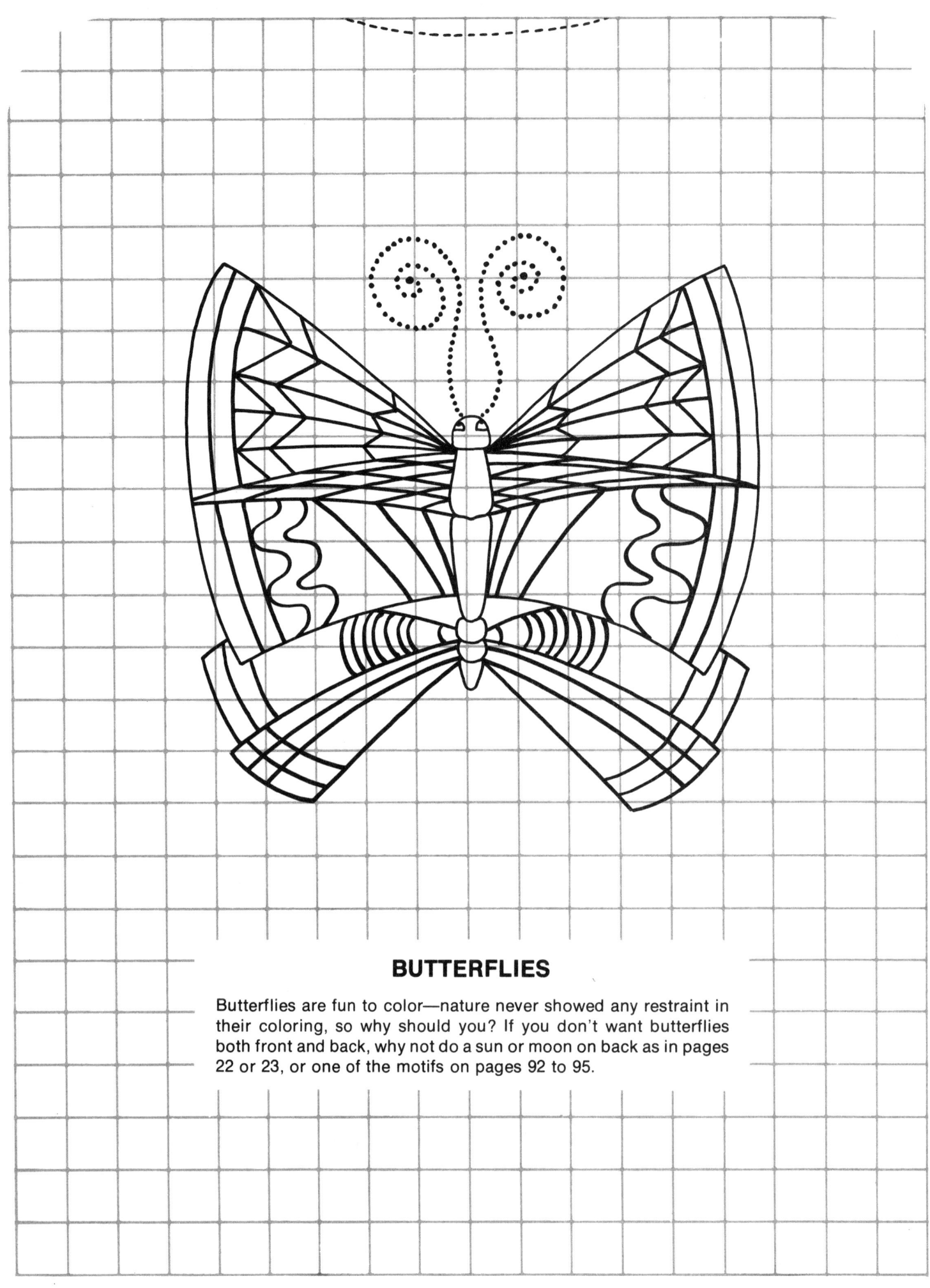

BUTTERFLIES

Butterflies are fun to color—nature never showed any restraint in their coloring, so why should you? If you don't want butterflies both front and back, why not do a sun or moon on back as in pages 22 or 23, or one of the motifs on pages 92 to 95.

Each square equals one inch

PAINT BY NUMBERS

This paint-by-numbers shirt would make a great gift for a friend who's never outgrown coloring books. Don't color in the drawing (except the frame), but do color in the numbered squares using colors that conform to the numbers in the drawing. For example:

1: cream color   5: light green   9: dark blue
2: pale yellow   6: dark green   10: pale gray
3: red   7: yellow   11: brown
4: beige   8: light blue   12: dark gray

For the back, use five of the colors from the numbered squares to do the strokes and squiggles made by the various pens, brushes, pencils and markers.

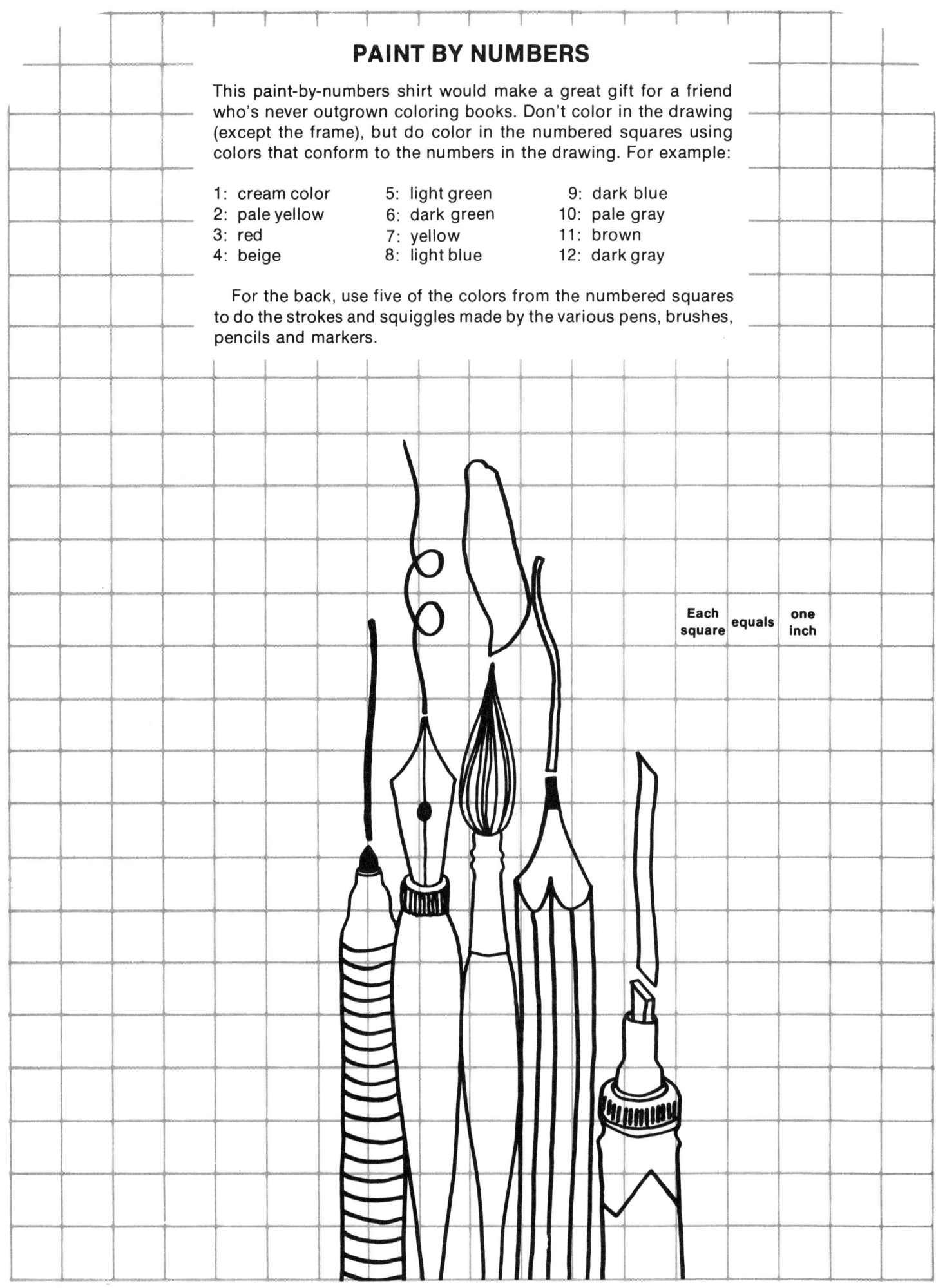

Each square equals one inch

Zippers and Pockets and Sleeves and Toggles and Collars and Ties and Buttons and Bows

In this section you'll find parts of pieces which you can substitute for those shown in the previous shirt patterns, or you can make them the basis of shirts you can design yourself.

Try a T-shirt with a zip-up front, or a toggle closing for when you'd like a little pomp and circumstance. There are buttons for fancy button downs, pockets to hold your wallet and comb, cuff designs to use on long-sleeved shirts, fancy collars and lots of ties.

Design motifs which you can use in combination with these elements are found in the following section, pages 88 to 101.

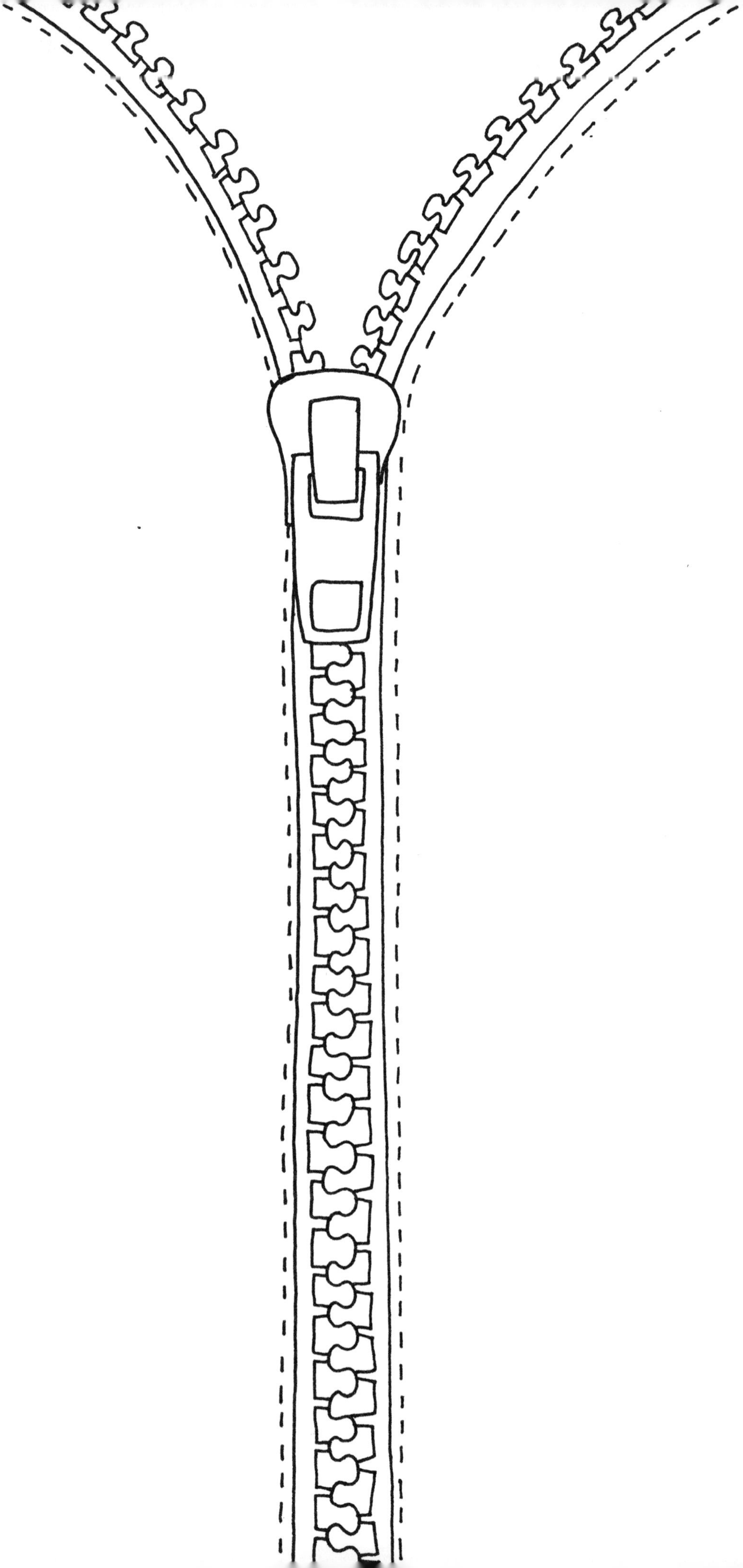

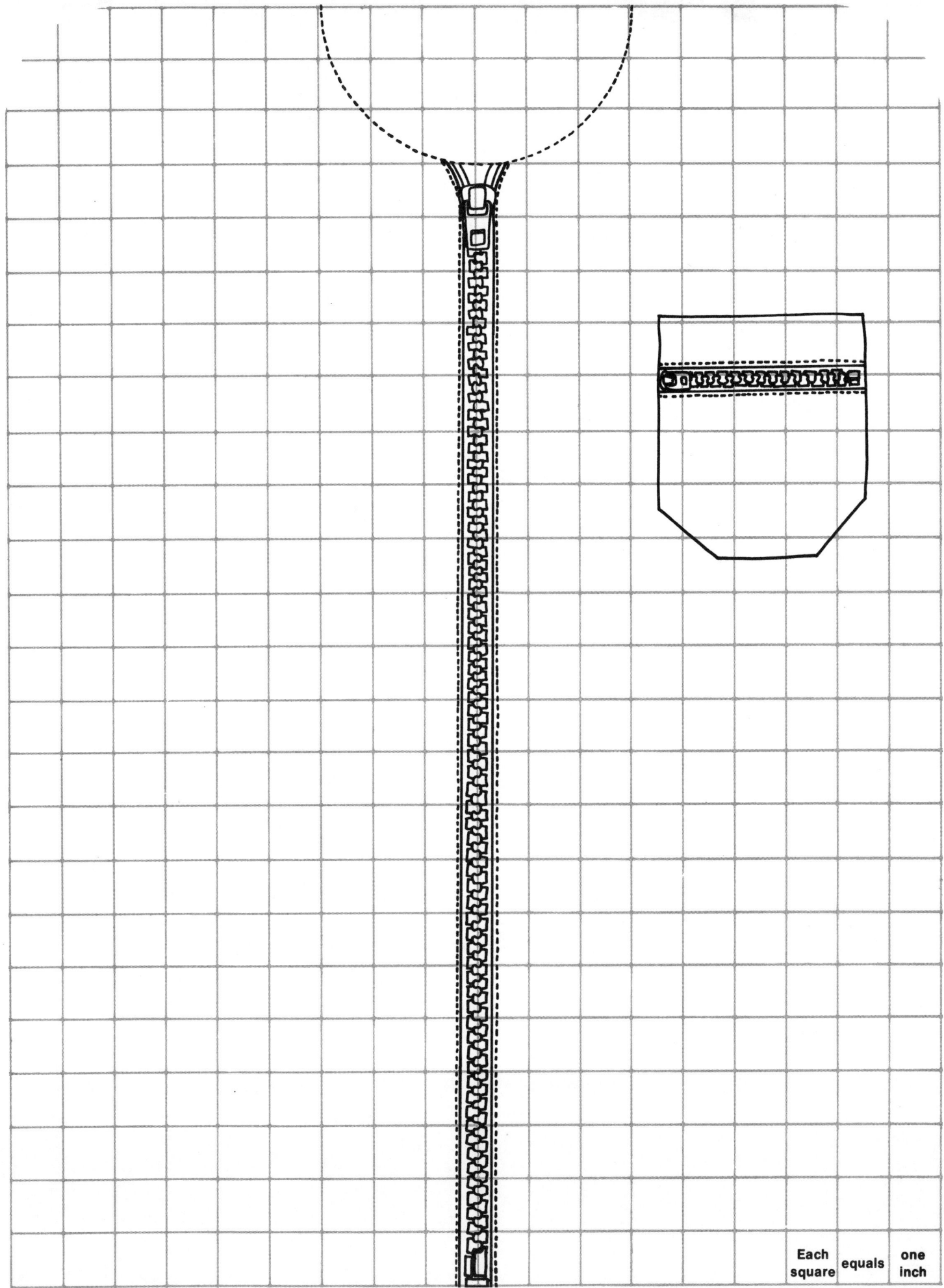

Each square equals one inch

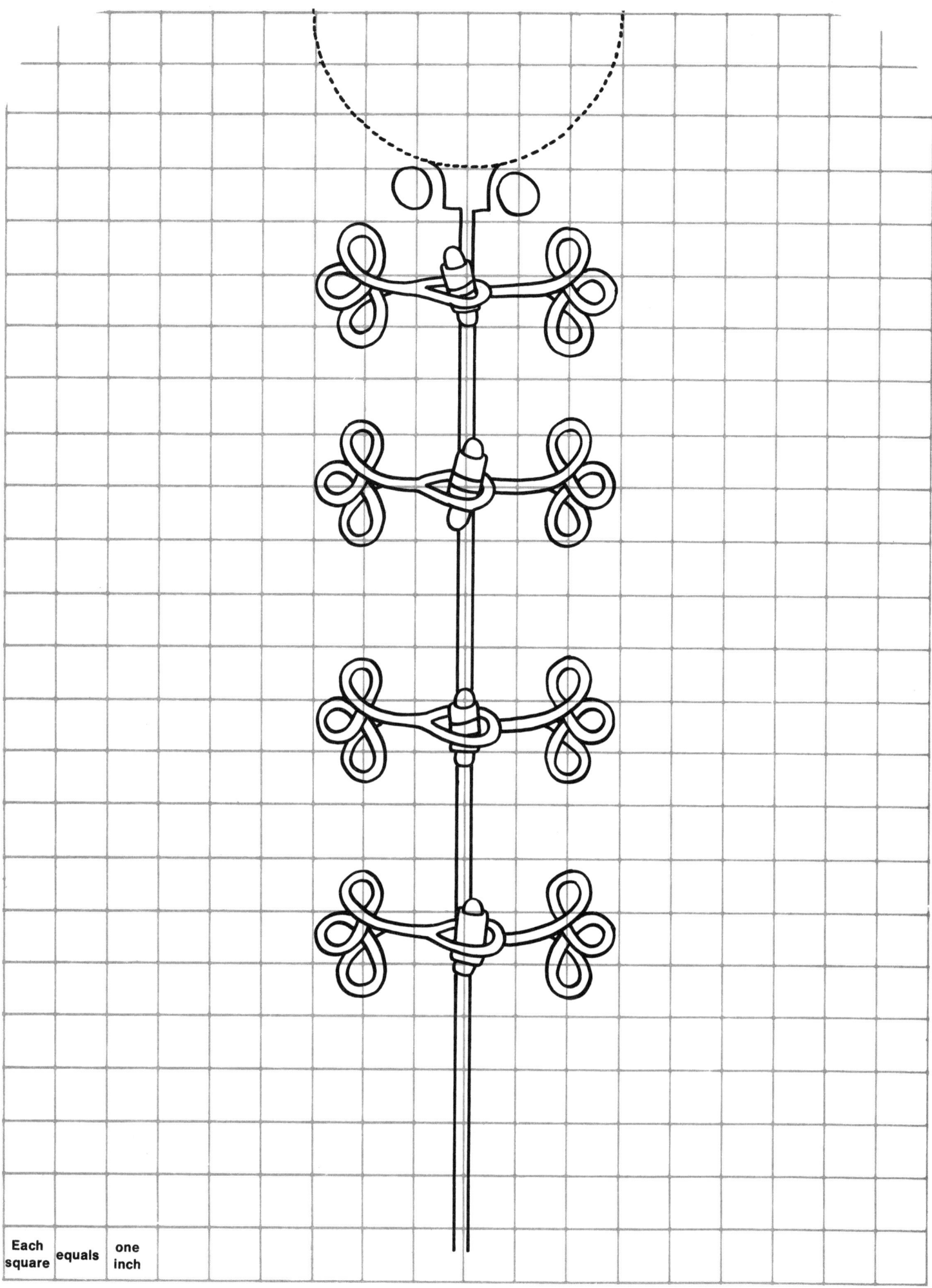

Each square equals one inch

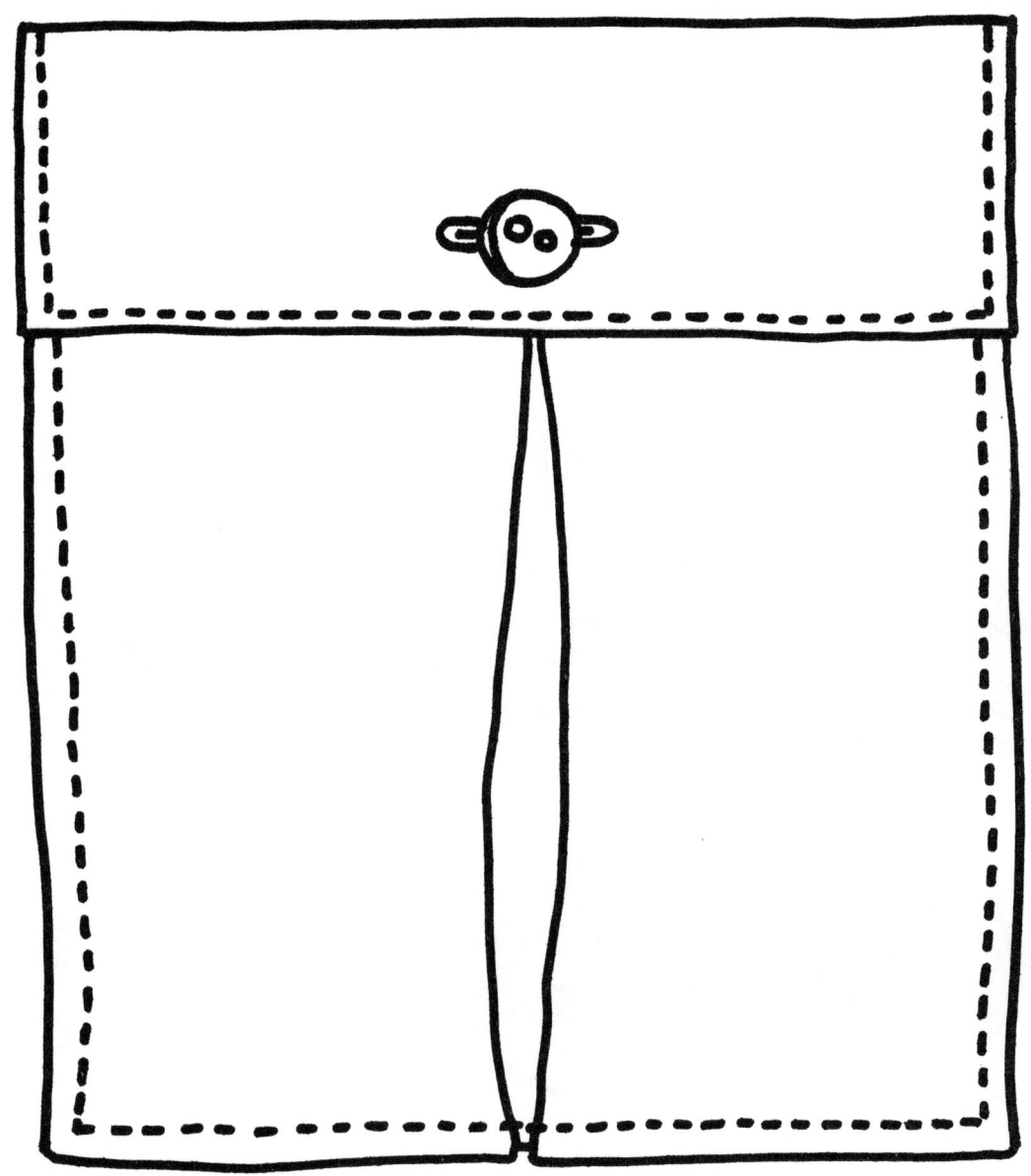

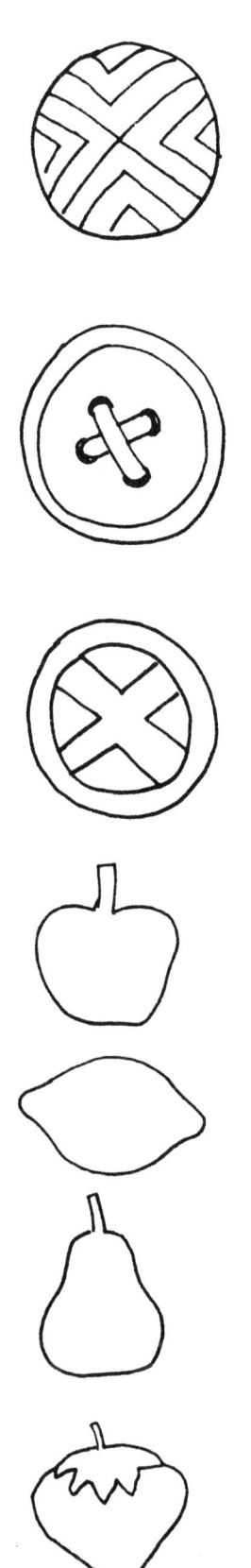

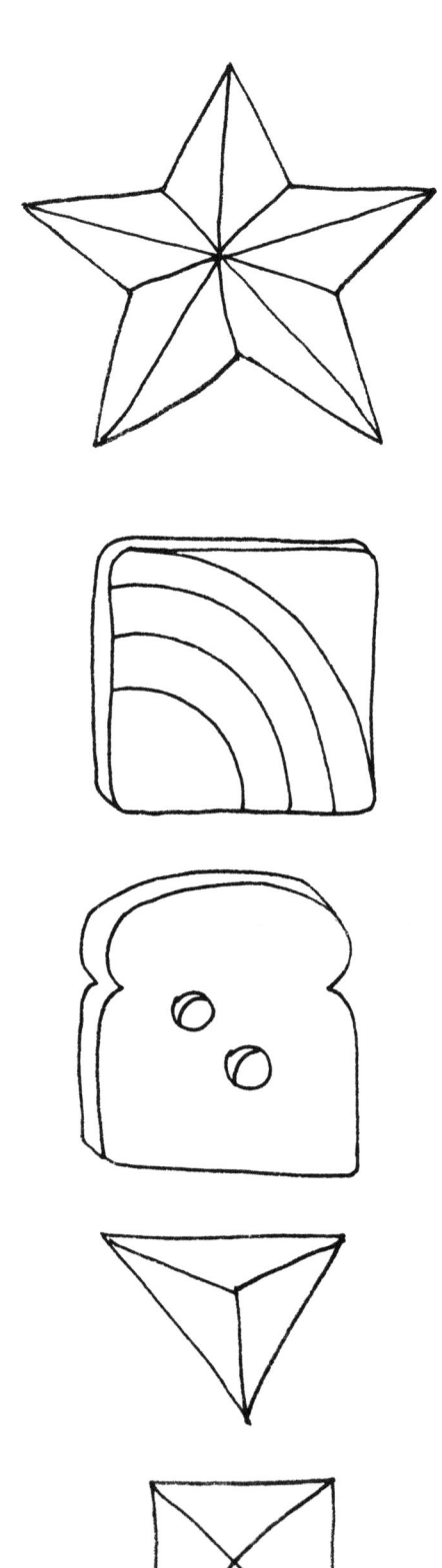

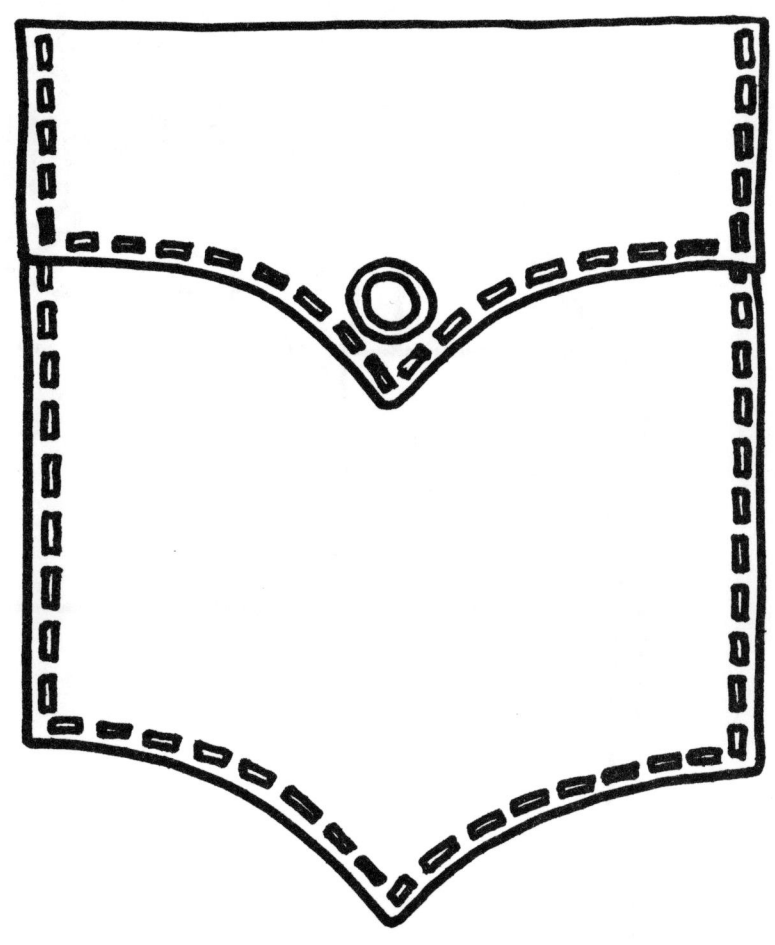

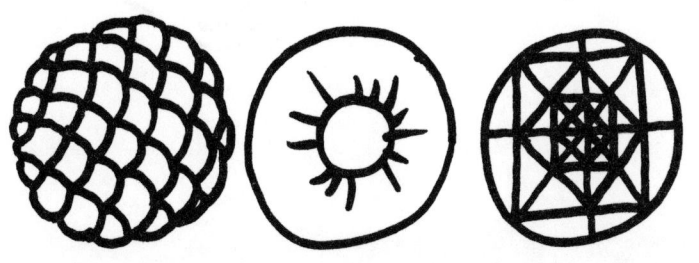

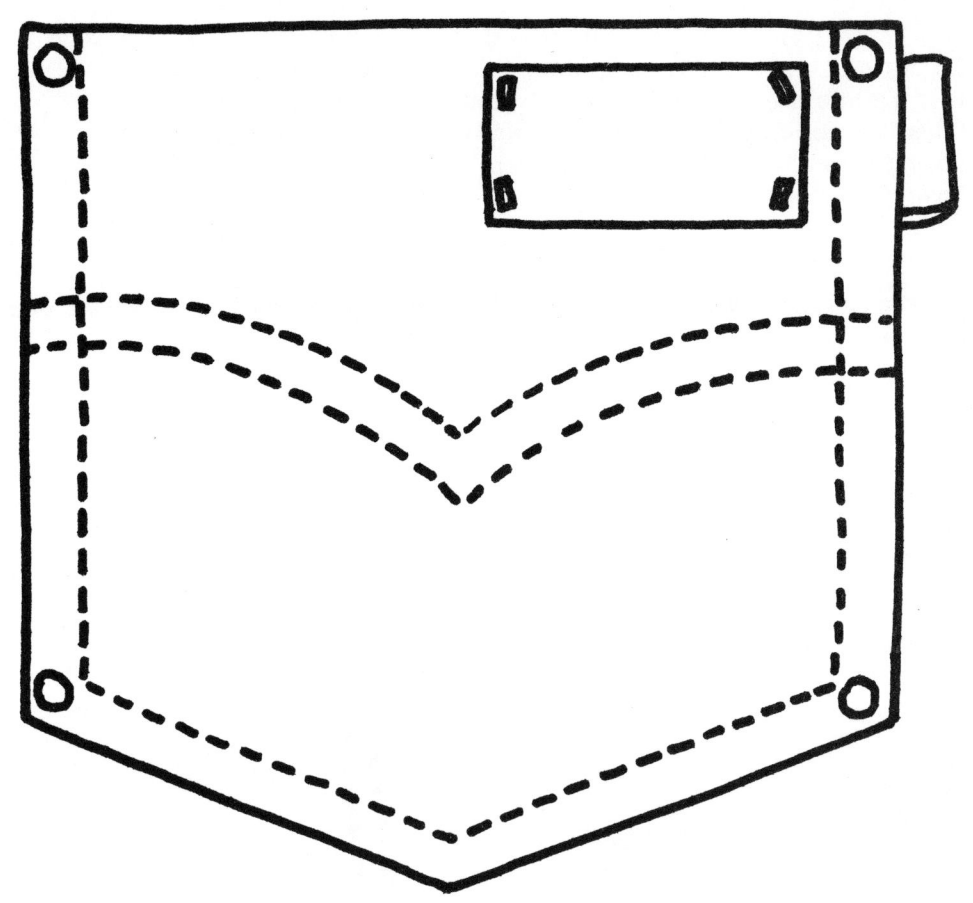

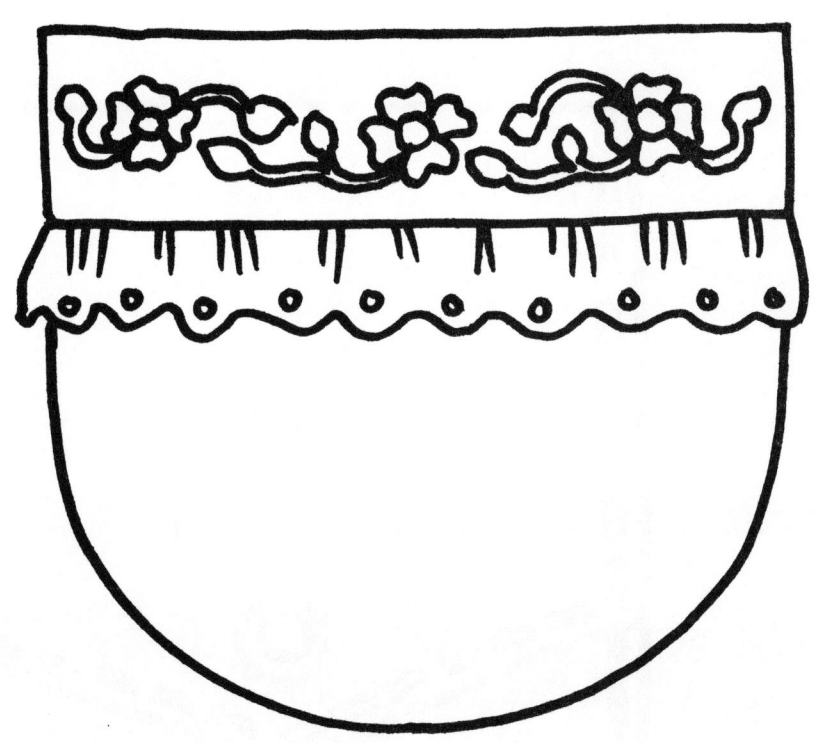

To draw and color cuffs, roll an ample section of newspaper and insert it into the opening of your shirt sleeve, adjusting it until it pulls the fabric tight enough to draw on. Be sure to position the design carefully, so that it falls properly when worn. Patterns are given for both left and right sleeves—don't mix them up.

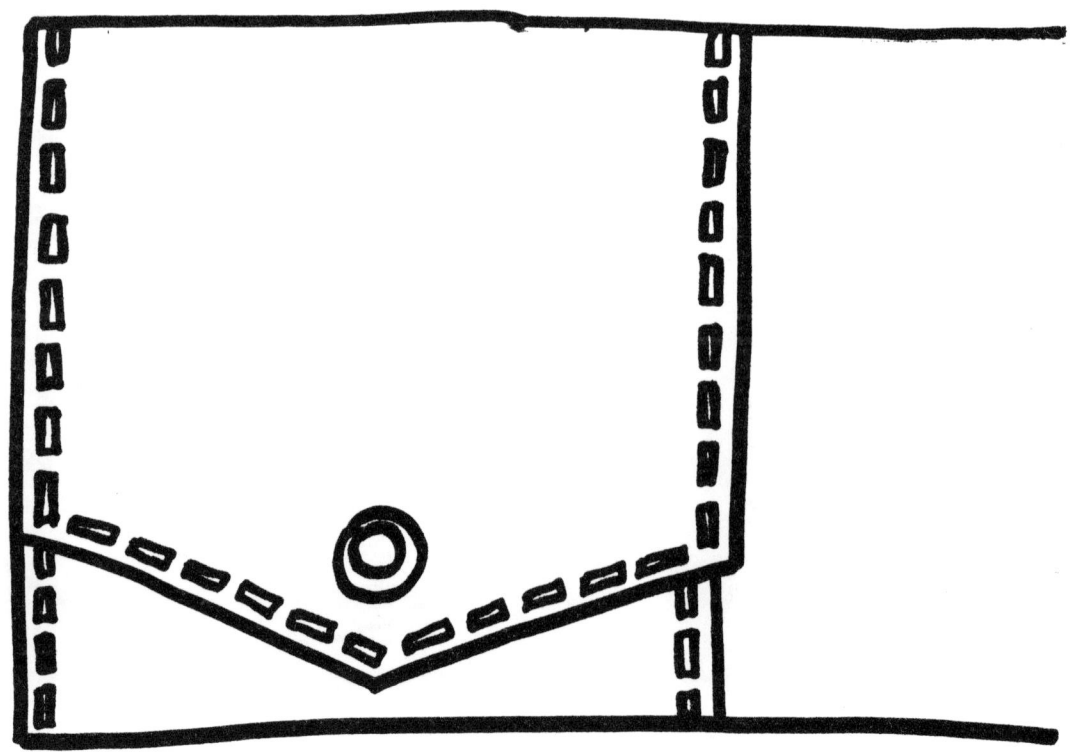

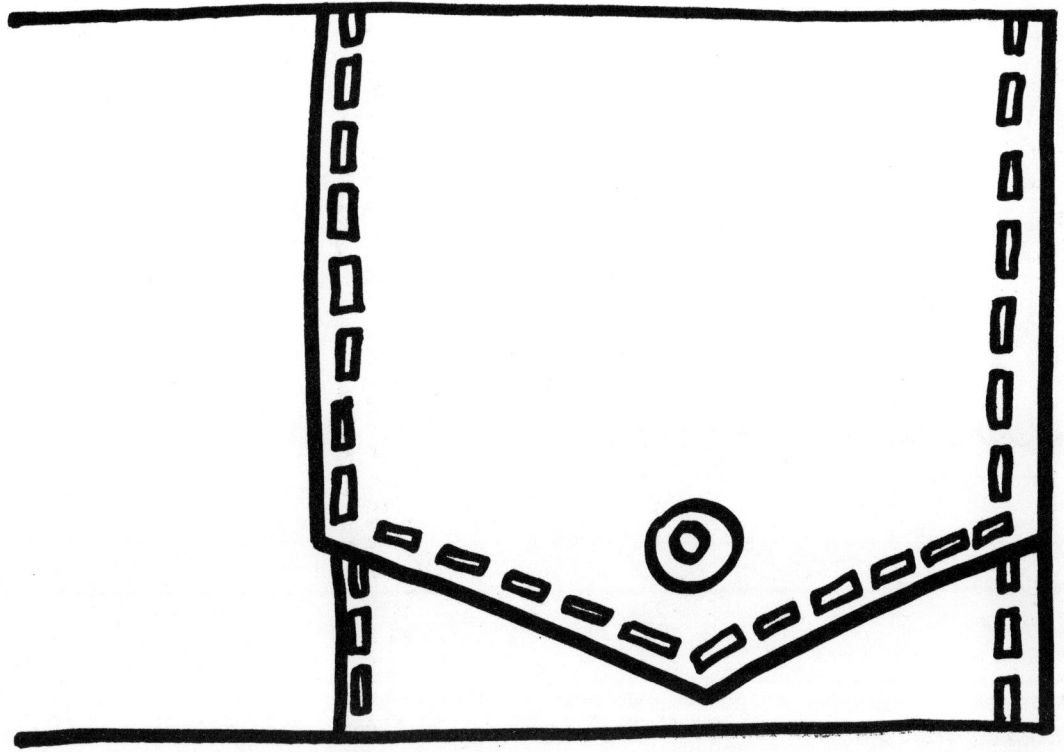

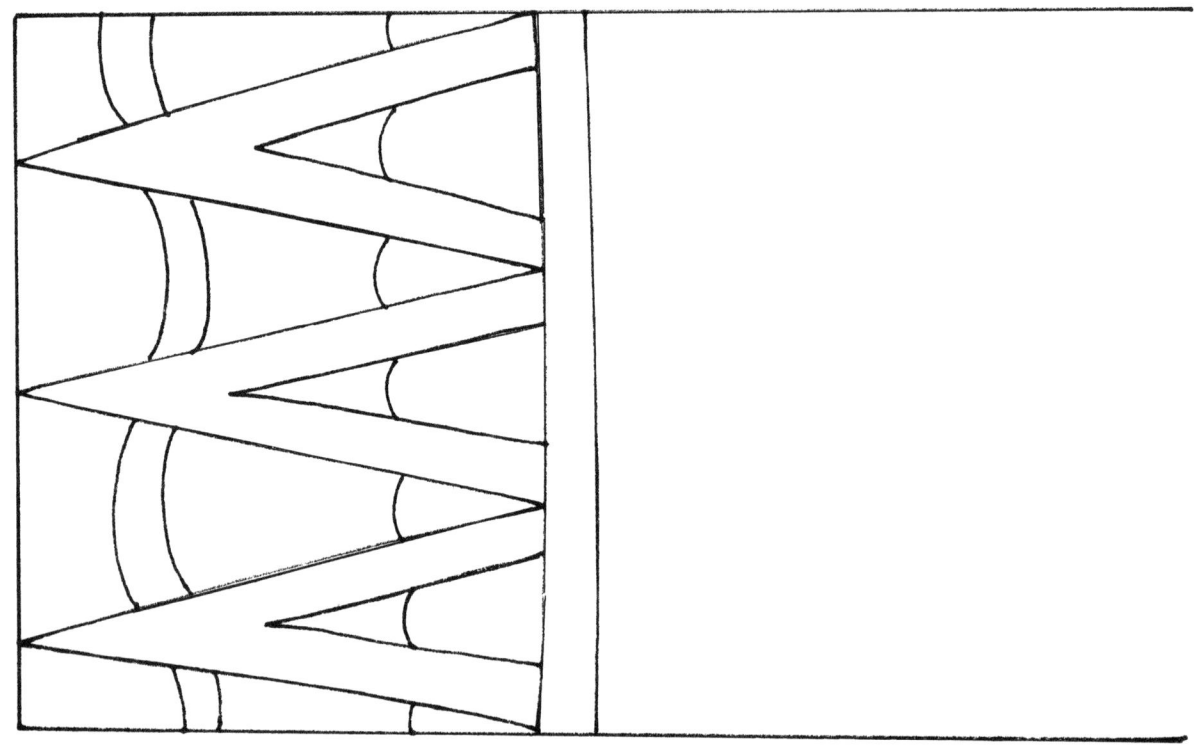

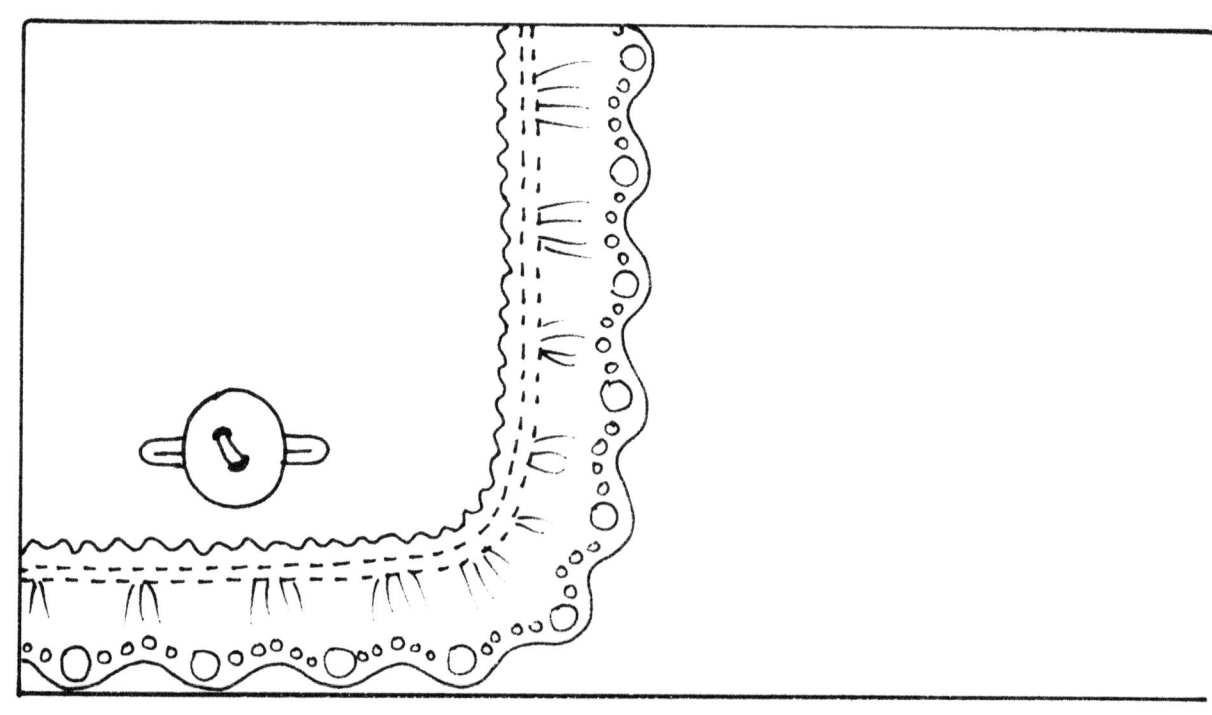

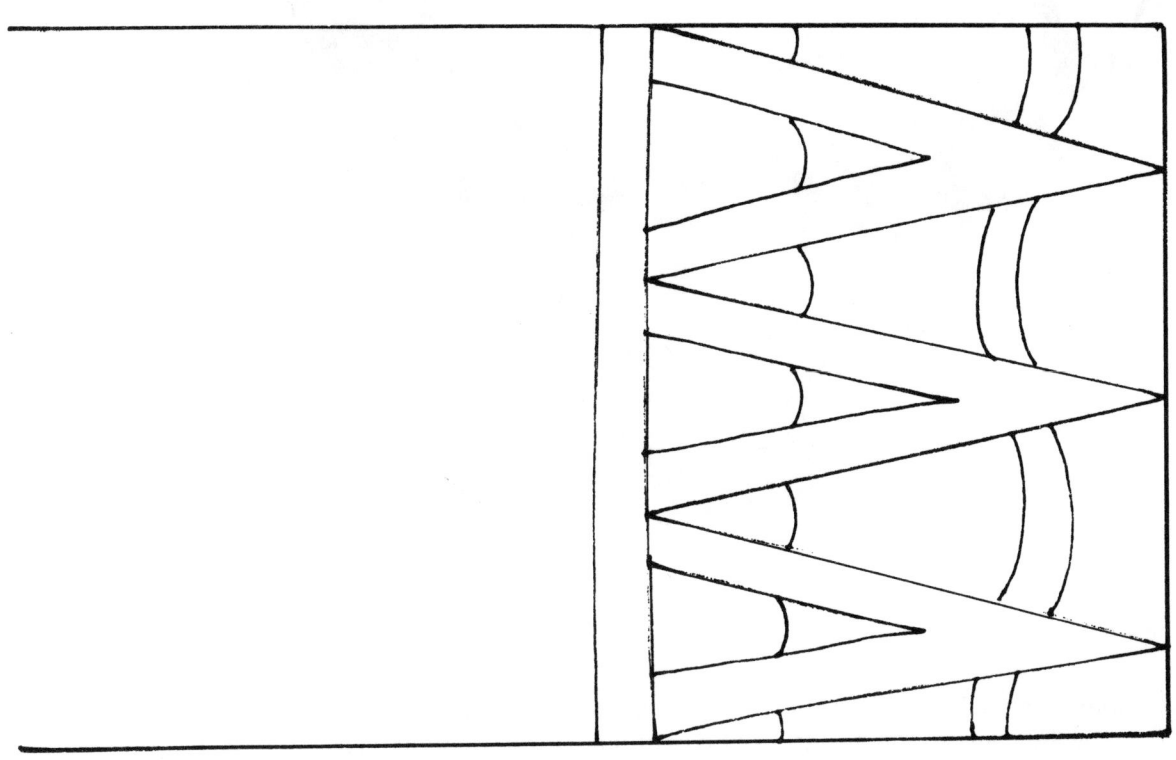

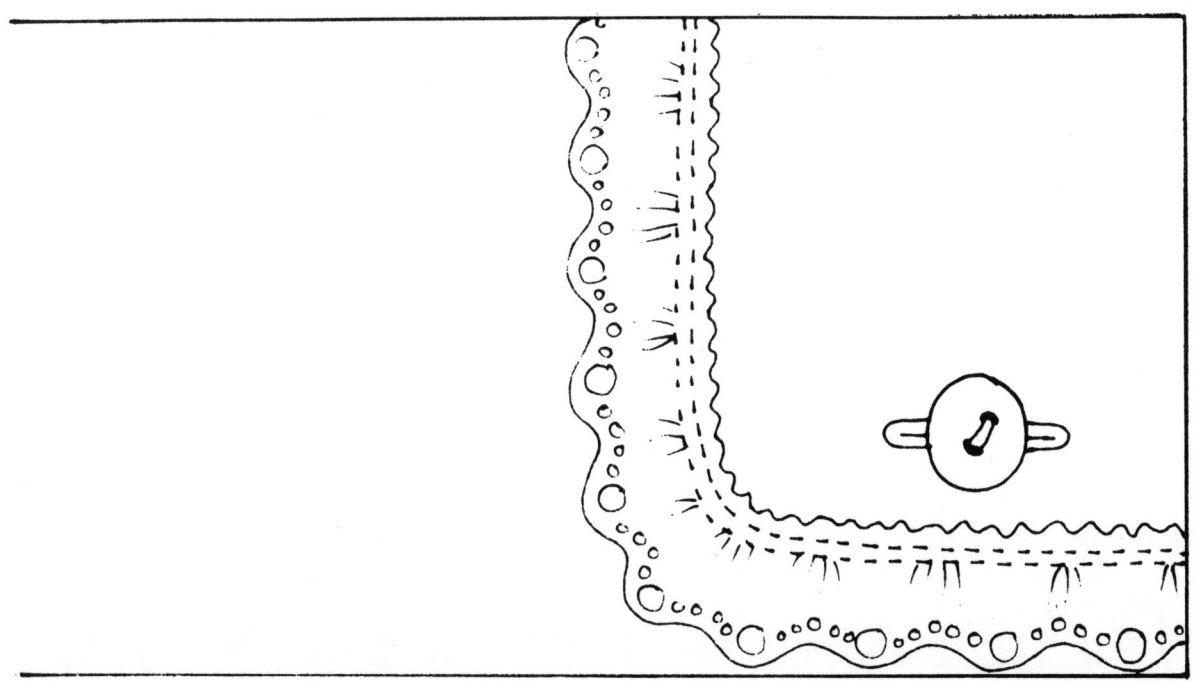

Collar motifs like the one shown above make an interesting T-shirt all by themselves; the design can be continued around to the back of the shirt. Try making collars in other patterns such as Indian necklaces, Mexican motifs, embroidered designs, etcetera.

Each square equals one inch

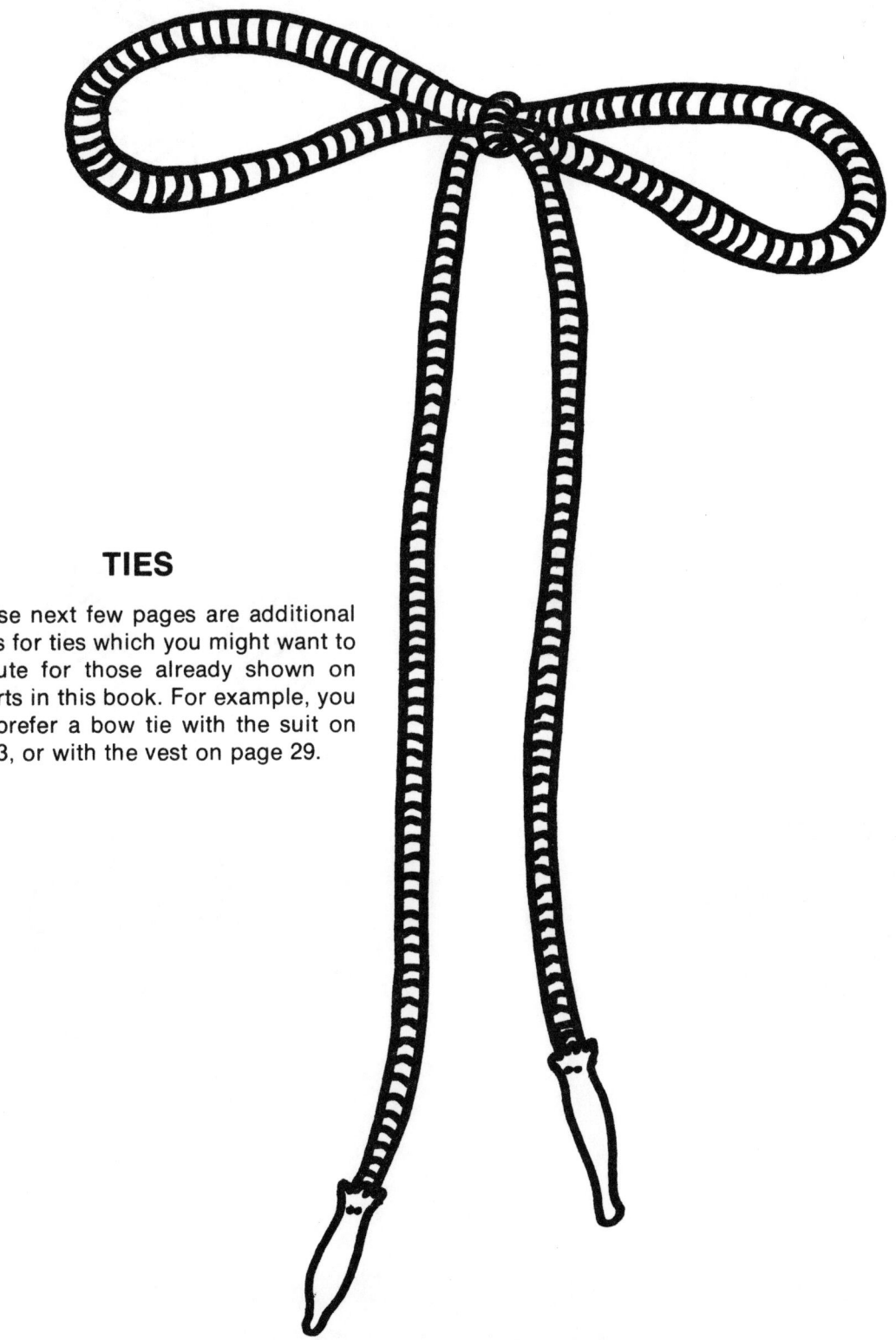

TIES

On these next few pages are additional designs for ties which you might want to substitute for those already shown on the shirts in this book. For example, you might prefer a bow tie with the suit on page 33, or with the vest on page 29.

The anonymous face in the tie on the right could be filled in to caricature the wearer, and the tie on the left calls out for a message in the center space.

Each square equals one inch

On the left, a Palm Beach tie, just the thing to wear with your old madras plaid Bermuda shorts. And on the right, a tie with tie clasp for the fastidious dresser.

Miscellaneous
Motifs and
Decorations

The full size designs on the following pages can be traced directly onto your T-shirt.

Several motifs could be combined on a shirt of your own design, or you can substitute these motifs on shirts in the earlier section of the book.

As a patriotic New Yorker, I couldn't resist starting right off with a Big Apple. It would go well with several of the shirts in the book —for example, you might substitute it for one side of the food shirt on pages 52 and 53.

How about having this snake slithering across the belly of your shirt? If you use friendly colors it won't look so menacing. Try combining it with the apple on page 89.

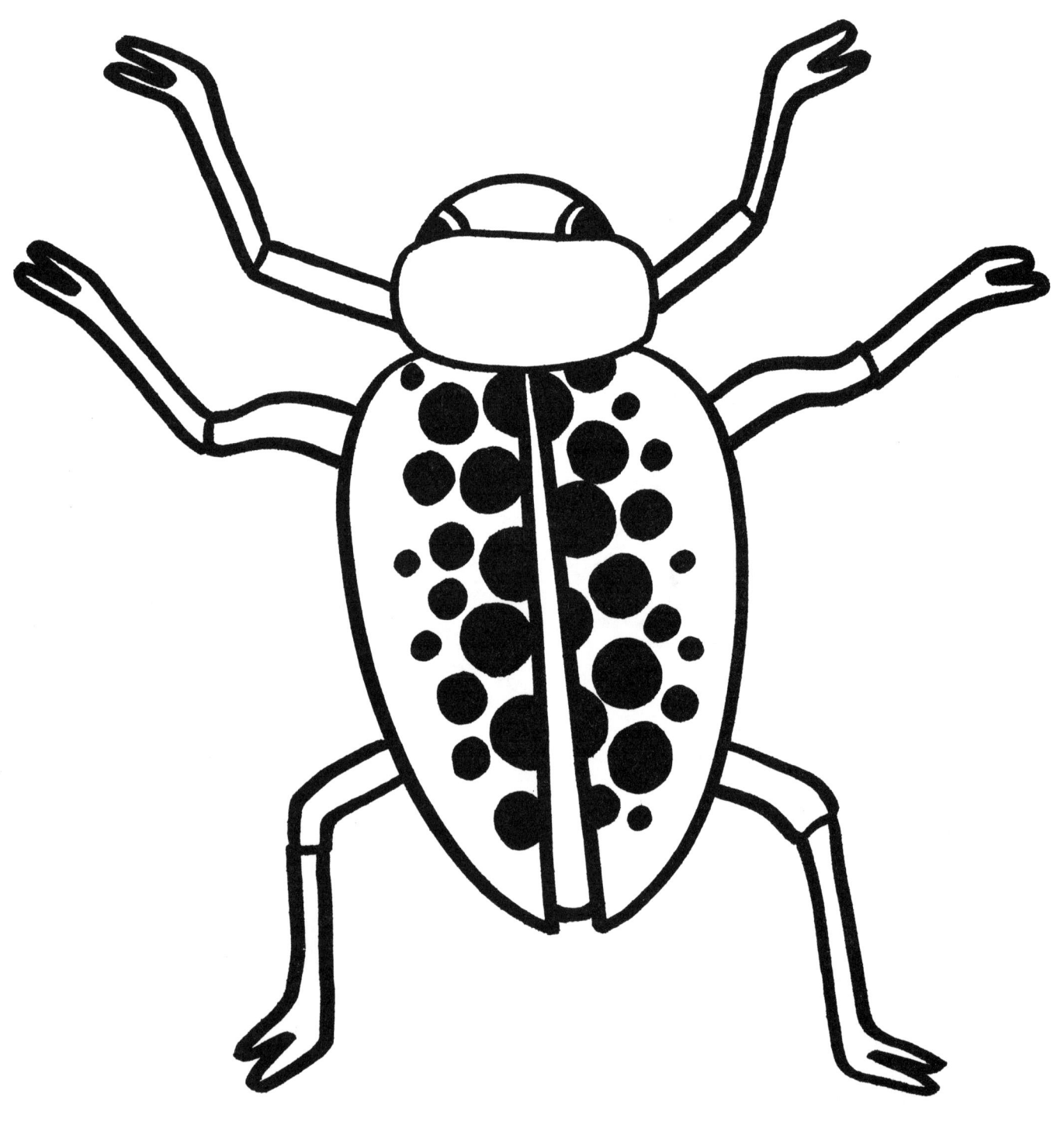

Here are a couple of bugs to crawl around a shirt. You might combine them with the butterflies on pages 64 and 65, or with the snake on 90.

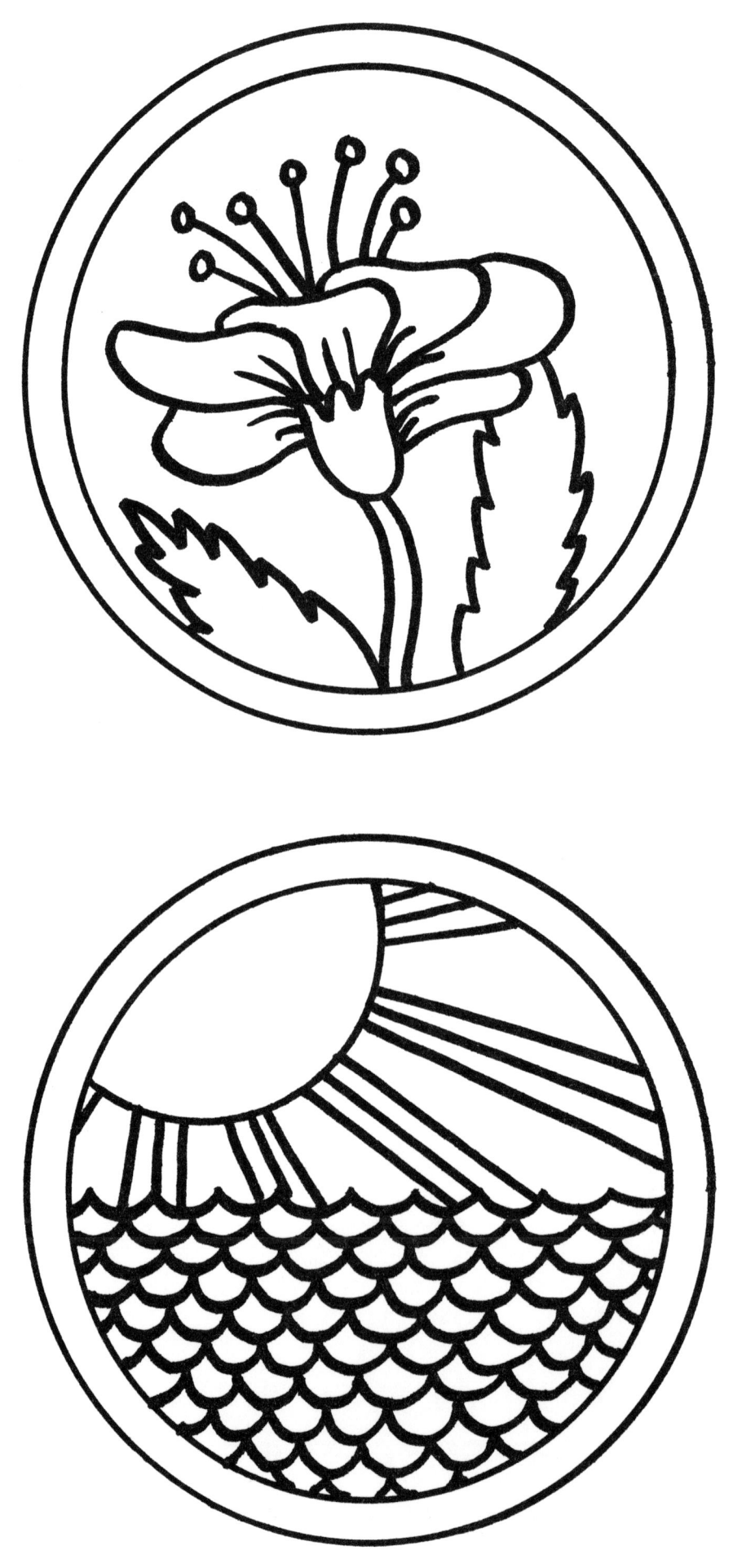

The circle motifs would look interesting in repeat patterns—four in a square, for example, or in a row across the front of a shirt.

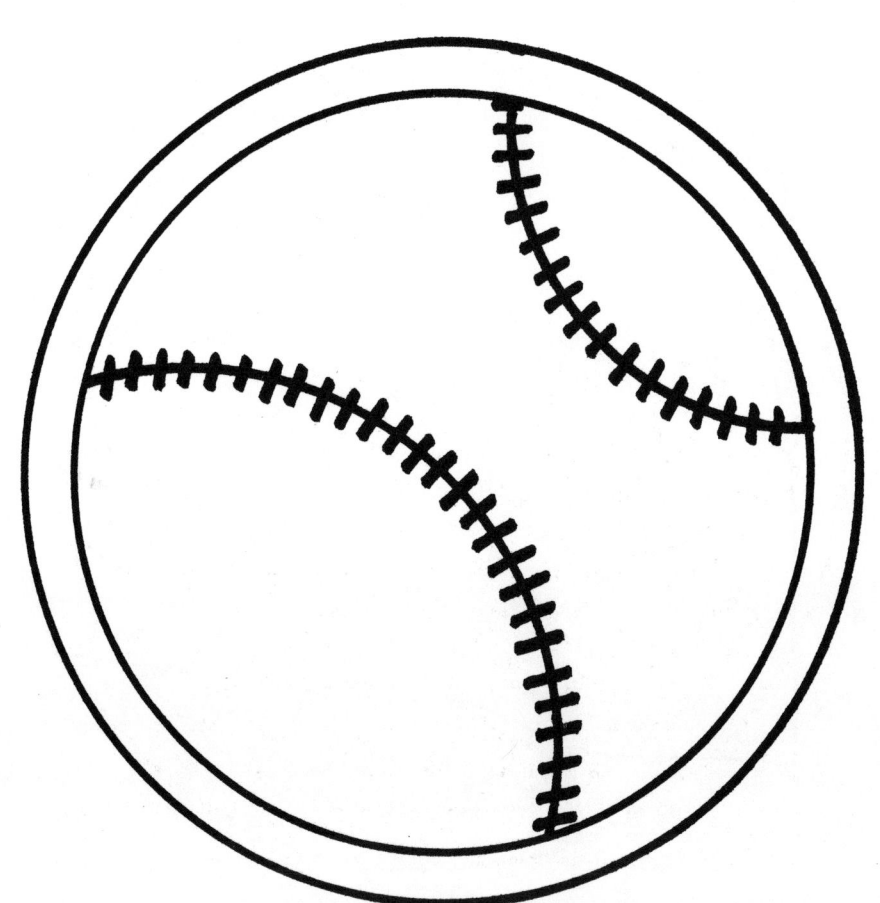

Be the first on your block with a T-shirt
on your T-shirt.

This ice cream soda will look yummy on your tummy. You might like to try it with a hot dog on the back (page 52) for a well-balanced meal.

If you don't have a three-piece Panama suit, try this for a refreshing summer look.

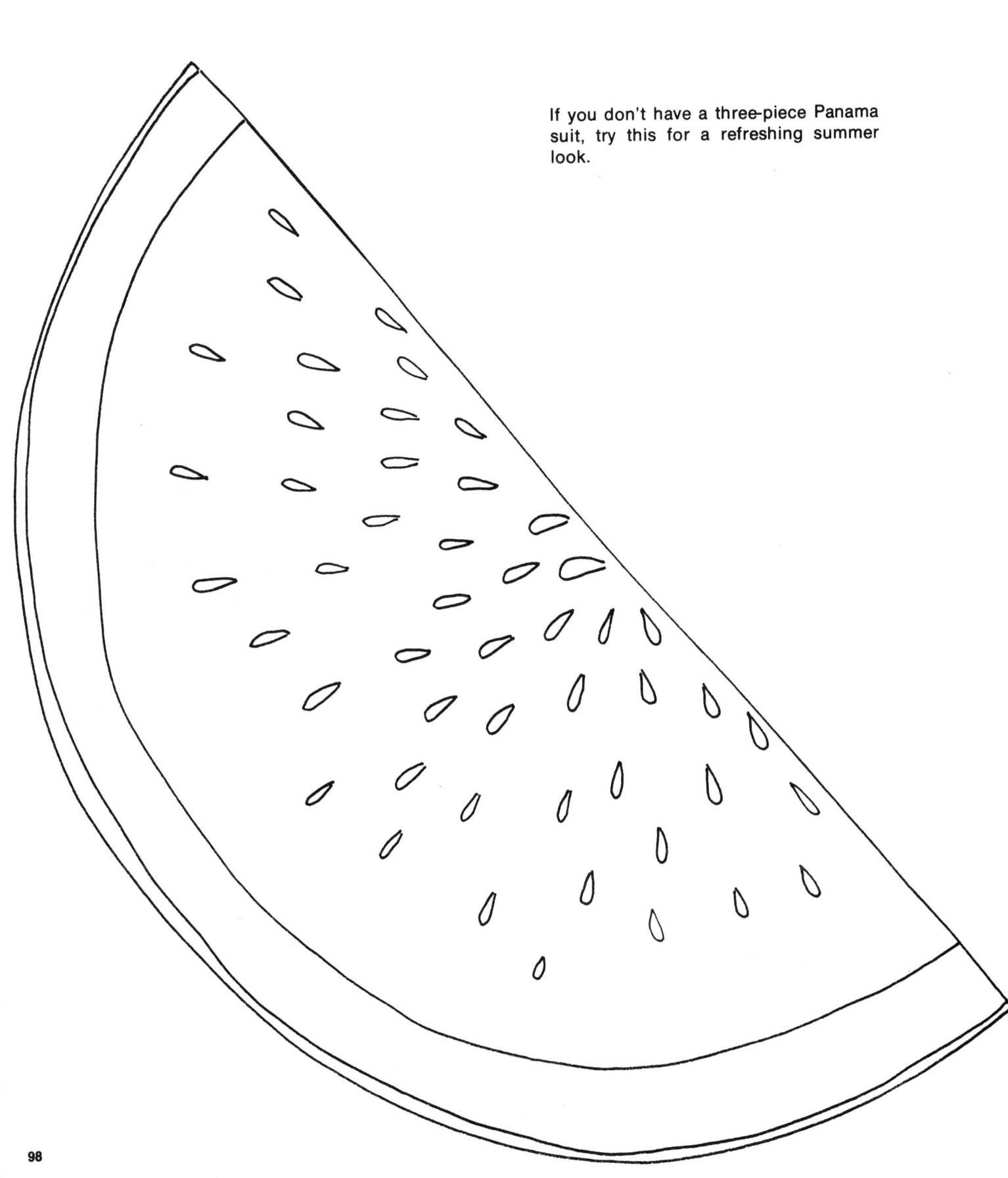

How about a patriotic T-shirt—A Bicentennial motif on the front
(page 109) and mom's apple pie on the back.

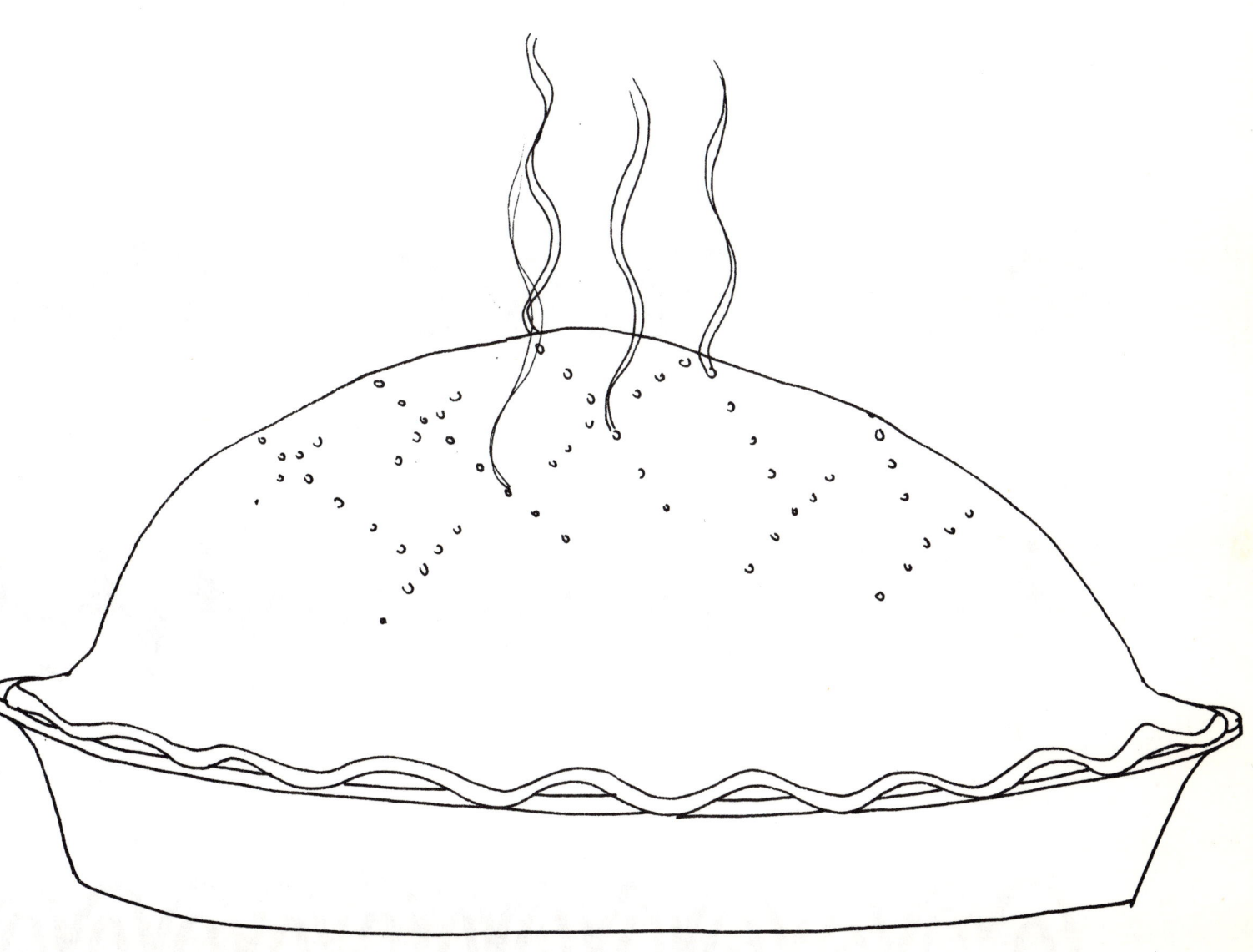

These border motifs are good for added decoration on simple shirts. Use them as borders around the bottom, around a collar, or to frame a "message." Or repeat several rows for an allover pattern.

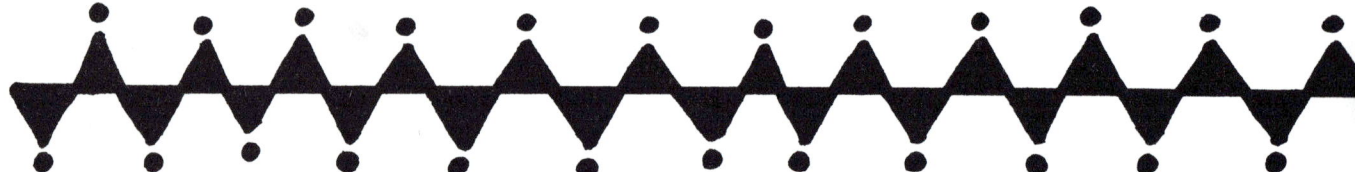

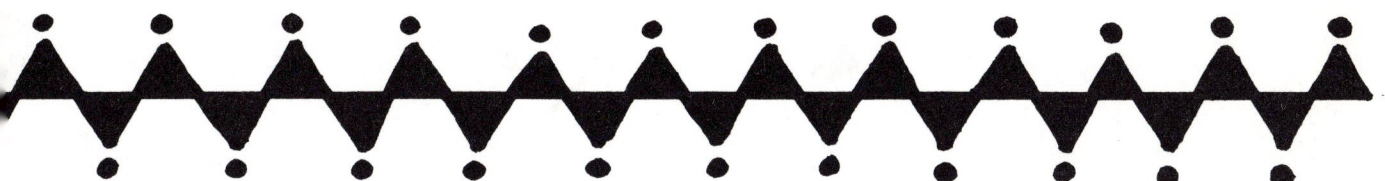

Kid Stuff

Kids and T-shirts are a natural combination. Here are some motifs especially for children's T-shirts, which can be directly traced from the patterns.

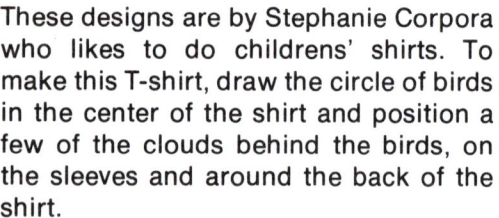

These designs are by Stephanie Corpora who likes to do childrens' shirts. To make this T-shirt, draw the circle of birds in the center of the shirt and position a few of the clouds behind the birds, on the sleeves and around the back of the shirt.

Position the gorilla design (also by Stephanie Corpora) at the bottom of the shirt and then continue the grass all the way around the bottom as a border.

Any child would love a T-shirt with one of
these motifs on it, and his team's name
or initial on the back. (Or use the "A" for
"Athlete" on page 34.)

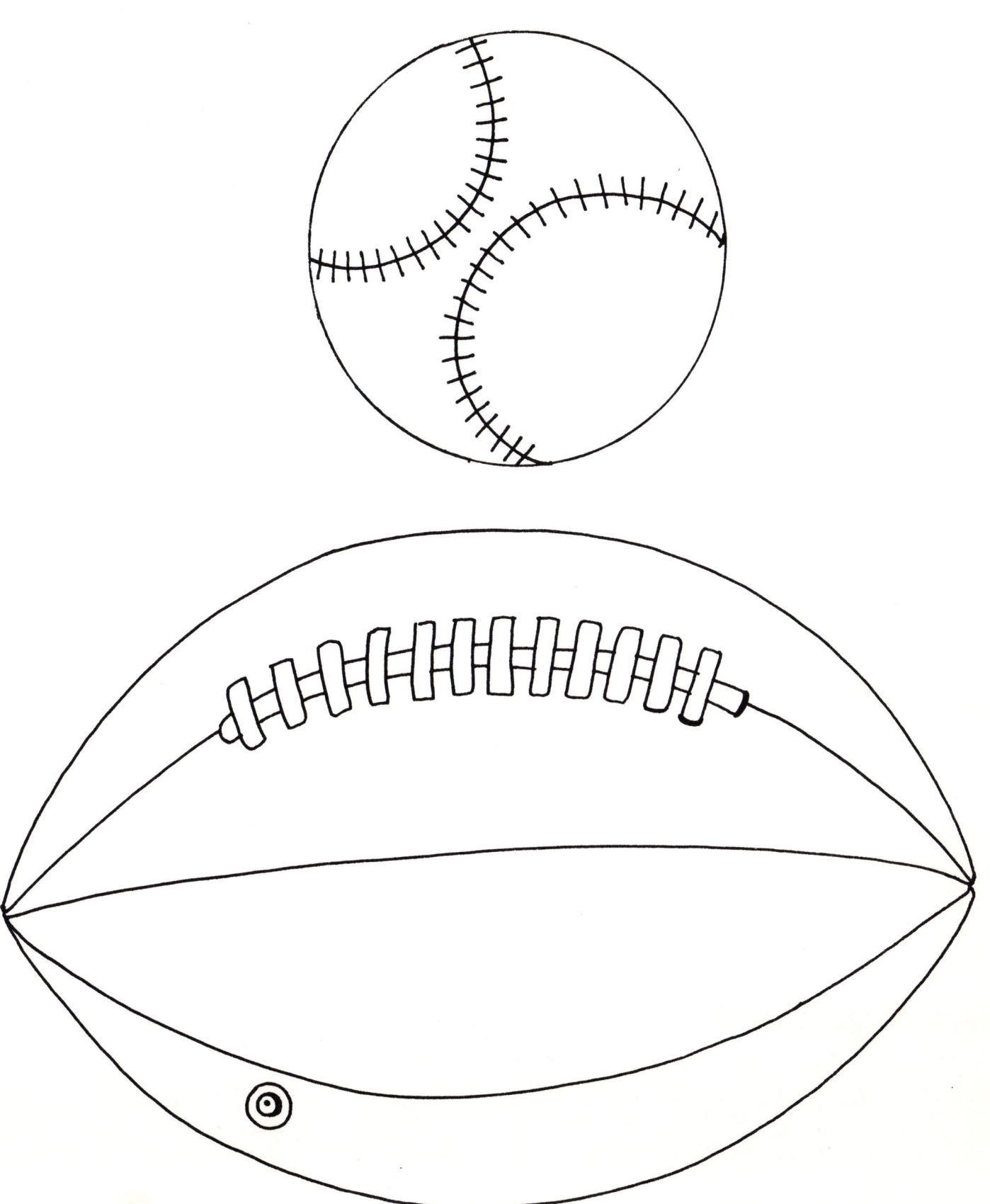

Timely T-shirts

T-shirts make wonderful gifts for special occasions. Christmas, Congratulations, Happy Birthday, Valentine's Day, and the biggest birthday of them all—the Bicentennial—are given here. If Groundhog Day's your thing, you're on your own.

Here are motifs for congratulations (on whatever) and birthdays. The congratulations motif is positioned properly for the neckline of the shirt. You should line up the birthday motif with the bottom, or you can draw the balloons higher and continue the strings down to the bottom.

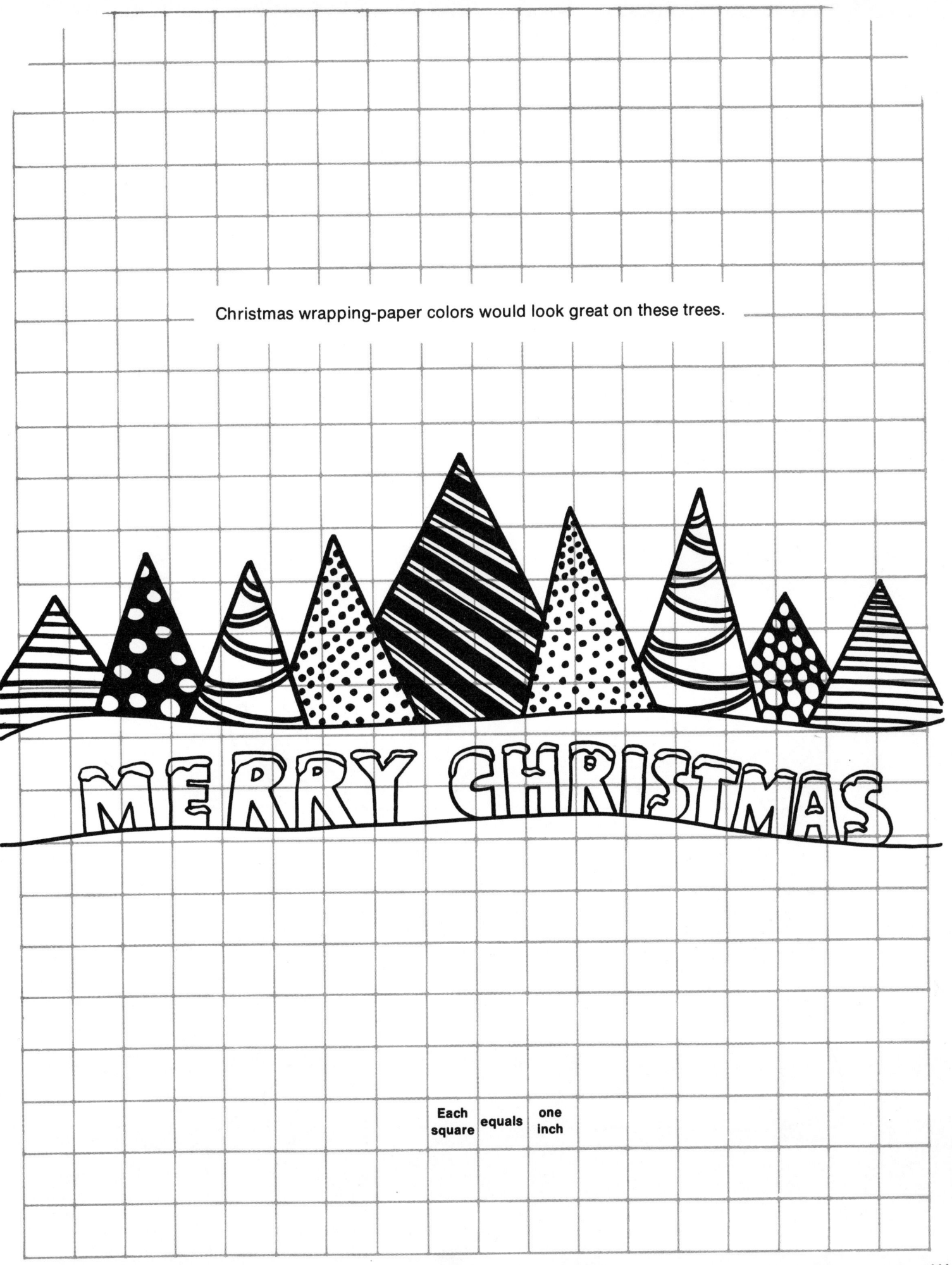

Christmas wrapping-paper colors would look great on these trees.

Each square equals one inch

Endearment of your choice goes here.

ABC's
and
123's

For messages, monograms, mottos, endearments, declarations, warnings, writs, well-chosen words, announcements, identifications. Say it with markers!

You can trace your message on tracing paper, using the alphabet of your choice. Move the tracing paper around to position each letter. Then transfer it to your T-shirt.

A B C D
E F G H
I J K L
M N O
P Q R S

T U V W

X Y Z !

1 2 3 ?

4 5 6 "

7 8 9 0 $

ABCDE

FGHIJK

LMNO

PQRSS

TUVW

XYZ

¢$12345

67890

ABCD
EFGHI
JKLM
NOPQR

STUV
WXYZ
12345
67890

aabbcc

ddeeff

ggghh

iijjkk

lmnopp

qqrrss

ttuvwx

yyz

A B C D

E F G H

I J K L

L M N

O P Q R

S T U V

W X Y

Z

1 2 3 4 5

6 7 8 9 0

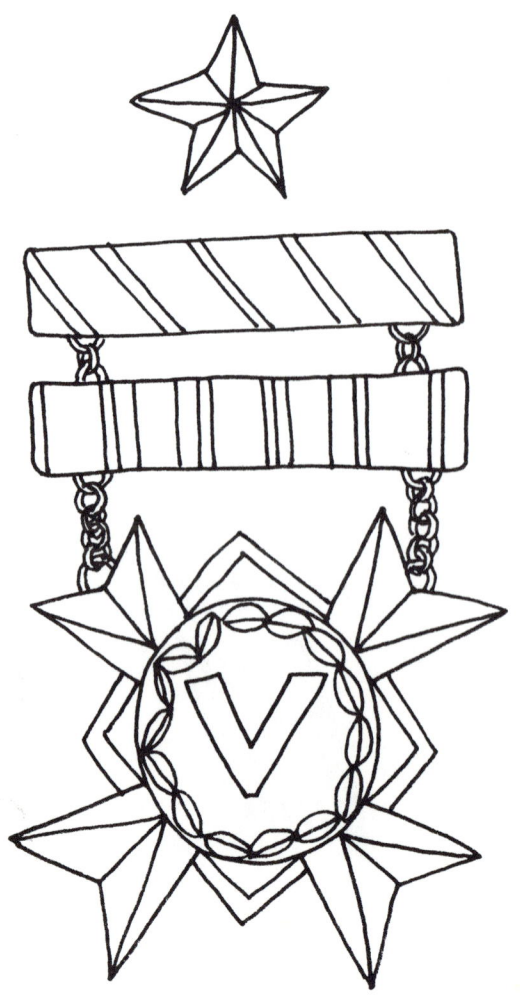

A B C D E E E

F G H I J K L

M N O P Q

R S T U V

W X Y Z

ABOUT THE AUTHOR

LAURA TORBET was art director for a New York firm before starting her own graphic design studio. She is the author of **Macramé You Can Wear**, and **Clothing Liberation**, and co-author of **The Leather Book.** She is currently working on an encyclopedia of crafts.

And as we all can see, she is tired of drawing T-shirts for now and has probably gone off for a bite to eat, or to bed, or to play tennis, or to Pago Pago. . . .

Each square equals one inch